HARD FRUIT

D1079696

Published by Methuen 2000

1 3 5 7 9 10 8 6 4 2

First published in Great Britain in 2000 by Methuen Publishing Limited
215 Vauxhall Bridge Road, London SW1V 1EJ

Methuen Publishing Limited Reg. No. 3543167

A CIP catalogue record is available from the British Library

ISBN 0 413 74820 0

Typeset by SX Composing DTP, Rayleigh, Essex
Printed and bound in Great Britain by
Cox & Wyman Ltd, Reading, Berkshire

Hard Fruit

Jim Cartwright

Methuen

ROYAL COURT

Royal Court Theatre presents

HARD FRUIT

by **Jim Cartwright**

First performed at the Royal Court Jerwood Theatre Downstairs,
Sloane Square, London on 31 March 2000

HARD FRUIT

by **Jim Cartwright**

Cast in order of appearance
Choke **Nicholas Woodeson**
Sump **Richard Hope**
Mrs Kooee **Hilda Braid**
Yack **Barry Howard**
Silver **Gary Grant**
Friar Jiggle **Alan Gear**

Director **James Macdonald**
Designer **Rob Howell**
Lighting Designer **Howard Harrison**
Sound Designer **Paul Arditti**
Fight Choreographer **Geoff Thompson**
Choreographer **Stuart Hopps**
Assistant Choreographer **Elaine Tyler-Hall**
Casting Director **Lisa Makin**
Production Manager **Paul Handley**
Company Stage Manager **Cath Binks**
Stage Manager **Pea Horsley**
Deputy Stage Manager **Claire Impey**
Assistant Stage Manager **Adam Legah**
Assistant Designer **Peter Linley**
Assistant Director **Christiane Hille**
Costume Supervisor **Iona Kenrick**
Dialect Coach **Jeannette Nelson**
Company Voice Work **Patsy Rodenburg**
Indian Club Coach **Jackie Crosher**
Personal Trainer **Hugh Craig**
Massage **Sue Cook**
Set Construction **Souvenir Scenic Studios**

Royal Court Theatre wishes to thank the following for their help with this production:
The Peacock Gym, Discurio, Sansha UK Ltd, Freed of London, JD Beardmore & co ltd, Safeway Stores, Master Brew, Kettler GB ltd, Charlie Holland @ Circus Space, Lee Davis @ Willesden Judo Club, Rose Bruford College, Bodum UK, CSA Fitness, Brewsters, Thermos Ltd, Paul Magarity, Boots Chemists, Peter Jones, B&Q, Kwick Save, Sharp and Nicless, Bacofoil, Tesco's, Silk Landscapes, Pukka-Pies, Americanautoparts.
Wardrobe care by Persil and Comfort courtesy of Lever Brothers Ltd.

THE COMPANY

Jim Cartwright (writer)
For the Royal Court: Road, I Licked a Slag's Deodorant.
Other theatre includes: Bed, The Rise and Fall of Little Voice (RNT); Two (Bolton Octagon/Young Vic); Prize Night (Royal Exchange, Manchester). Television includes: Road, Vroom, June, Wedded. Radio: Baths.
Awards include: Samuel Beckett Award, Drama Magazine's Best New Play, Joint winner of the George Devine Award and Plays and Players award for Road. Golden Nymph Award for Best Film for Road. Manchester Evening News Best New Play Award for Two. Evening Standard Best Comedy Award 1992 and the Olivier Award for Best Comedy 1993 for The Rise and Fall of Little Voice.
As director: I Licked a Slag's Deodorant (Royal Court); Road (Royal Exchange, Manchester).

Paul Arditti (sound designer)
Paul Arditti has been designing sound for theatre since 1983. He currently combines his post as Head of Sound at the Royal Court (where he has designed more than 50 productions) with regular freelance projects.
For the Royal Court: Other People, Dublin Carol, Breath, Boom, The Kitchen, Rat in the Skull, Some Voices, Mojo, The Lights, The Weir. The Steward of Christendom, Shopping and Fucking, Blue Heart (co-productions with Out of Joint). The Chairs (co-production with Theatre de Complicite); The Strip, Never Land, Cleansed, Via Dolorosa, Real Classy Affair.
Other theatre includes: Our Lady of Sligo (RNT with Out of Joint); Some Explicit Polaroids (Out of Joint); Hamlet, The Tempest (RSC); Orpheus Descending, Cyrano de Bergerac, St Joan (West End); Marathon (Gate).
Musicals include: Doctor Dolittle, Piaf, The Threepenny Opera.
Awards include: Drama Desk Award for Outstanding Sound Design 1992 for Four Baboons Adoring the Sun (Broadway).

Hilda Braid
Theatre includes: Waltz of the Torreadors (Criterion); The Iceman Cometh (Arts); The London Cuckolds (RNT); The Price of Meat (Nuffield); Peace in Our Time (tour); Habeas Corpus (Birmingham Stage Company); When We Are Married (Birmingham Rep); Under Milkwood. Other Women (Thorndike); Uncle Vanya (Hampstead); Enjoy (Manchester Library); The Crucible, On The Razzle, Blithe Spirit, Rose (Young Vic); Twelfth Night, Richard II, King John (RSC); She Stoops to Conquer (Chester Gateway); Pickwick! (Saville).
Television includes: Midsomer Murders, The Bill, After Eskimo Day, Kiss and Tell, Pirates, Dangerfield, Moving Story, Don't Tell Father, One Foot in the Grave, Stick With Me Kid, Anglo-Saxon Attitudes, Bazaar, Press Gang, Keeping It Clean, You Rang M'Lord, In Sickness and Health, Casualty, Citizen Smith, Hard Cases, The Bill, Brookside, The Bright Side, Rings on Their Fingers, Campaign, Chester Mystery Plays.
Films includes: Strong Boys, Douglas The Flour Baby, Mrs Dalloway, 101 Dalmations, Scrooge, The Wildcats of St Trinians, Dick Turpin, Killer's Moon, Aqua Velva 'Le Coq', Fantasy of Light.

Alan Gear
Theatre includes: Prize Night (Royal Exchange, Manchester); The Rise and Fall of Little Voice, Maid Marian and Her Merry Men (Bristol Old Vic); Taking Steps, Merlin's Dream (Northcott, Exeter); Robin, Prince of Sherwood (Piccadilly /Tour); A Midsummer Night's Dream, Much Ado About Nothing, Jesus Christ Superstar (Wolsey, Ipswich); Old Time Music Hall, Baths and Beds (Octagon, Bolton); Amadeus (RNT); Jeanne (Sadlers Wells/Birmingham); A Man for All Seasons, A Christmas Carol, Jack and the Giant (Nottingham Playhouse); Jack and the Beanstalk, Shore Saints and Sea Devils (Library, Manchester); Joseph (tour).
Television includes: Brazen Hussies, The Knock, A Touch of Frost, Affairs of the Heart, Bottle Boys, The Bill, London's Burning.
Film includes: Harry's Dilemma.
Alan also runs a glass painting company in Manchester and his book "The Complete Guide to Glass Painting" is published in March.

Gary Grant
Theatre includes: The Power Of Love
(Southwark Playhouse); Jumpshot (Riverside
Studios); Picasso (Sadlers Wells); One Season's
King (The Lost Theatre); Fenn (Old Bull Arts
Centre); The Master Builder (Riverside Studios).
Television includes: Dangerfield, Hollyoaks,
Laundry Lane, The One, Quarantine.
Film includes: Spinning Candyfloss, Living Is
Round, Cops and Robbers, Logical Love Story.

Howard Harrison (lighting designer)
Theatre includes: Mamma Mia! (West End);
Private Lives, Sleep with Me, Look Back in
Anger (RNT); As You Like It, The Tempest,
Henry VIII, The Merchant of Venice, Timon of
Athens (RSC); Martin Guerre, Kat and the Kings,
Putting It Together (Broadway).
Opera includes: The Elixir of Love (ENO), La
Forza Del Destino (Kirov Quarantine).
Ballet includes: Romeo and Juliet, Swan Lake
(English National Ballet).
Future work includes: The Witches of Eastwick
(West End); As You Like It (RSC); Nabucco
(Metropolitan Opera); Mamma Mia! (Toronto
/Australia).
Awards include: Olivier Award nomination for
Best Lighting Designer 1997 and 1999.

Christiane Hille (assistant director)
Productions include: Prince Caspian (Step Up
Productions); Unusual Conduct (Garage
Theatre, Edinburgh); Marriage Play (Judi Dench
Theatre); Line, Spitting Daisies (New York); The
Cherry Orchard (Brighton Little Theatre); Angel
City, Awake and Asleep, Three Women
(University of Sussex).

Richard Hope
Theatre includes: War and Peace, Street of
Crocodiles, The Visit, Pravda, Hamlet, The
Government Inspector, Don Juan, Much Ado
About Nothing (RNT); The Park (RSC); Betrayal
(West Yorkshire Playhouse); Anna Karenina
(Shared Experience); The Gentleman from
Olmedo, Don Gil of the Green Britches (Gate);
Candida (Tour); The Third Policeman (ICA);
Accidental Death of an Anarchist (Belt and
Braces); The Hitchhiker's Guide to the Galaxy
(ICA); 1001 Nights with Le Grand Magic Circus
(Shaftesbury); The Warp (ICA/Roundhouse);
Mother Courage, The Seed (Birmingham Rep);
Romeo and Juliet (Shaw Theatre).
Television includes: Rhona, Happy Birthday
Shakespeare, Midsomer Murders, Reach for the
Moon, Casualty, Children of the New Forest,
The Demon Headmaster, Bramwell, A Perfect
State, Jackanory, The Vet, Peak Practice, Band of
Gold, Tears Before Bedtime, The Riff Raff
Element, Children Crossing, Victoria Wood,

Playhouse, Happy Families, Casualty of War, A
Piece of Cake, Burning Ambition, Saturday
Sunday Monday, Brideshead Revisited.
Film includes: The Last Post, Antonia and Jane,
Bellman and True, See You at Wembley Frankie
Walsh, Laughterhouse, French Lieutenant's
Woman.
Awards include: Oscar for Best Short Film for
See You at Wembly Frankie Walsh.
Radio includes: Decameron, Missing the
Melody, People Like Us, To the Wedding.
Associate member of Theatre de Complicite
and Shared Experience. Associate director:
Anna Karenina (Shared Experience).

Stuart Hopps (choreographer)
Theatre includes: Katherine Howard
(Chichester); The Betrayal of Nora Blake
(Jermyn Street Theatre); Chips With Everything
(RNT); Who's Afraid of Virginia Wolf (Almeida);
A Satire of Four Estaites (Wildcat Productions):
Elizabeth (Ginza Saison Theatre, Japan); The
Painter of Dishonour (RSC); The Big Picnic (The
Tramshed); The Rocky Horrors Show (National
Tour); Medea (Barcelona Olymplad Culturel).
Television includes: The Passion; Class Act, Six
Characters In Search of an Author, Seekers.
Film includes: Love's Labour's Lost, Amy
Foster, Wings of a Dove, Hamlet, Twelfth
Night, Othello, Sense and Sensibility,
Carrington, Frankenstein, Much Ado About
Nothing.
Opera includes: The Silver Tassie (English
National Opera); Cunning Little Vixen (Royal
Opera House/English National Opera); The
Indian Queen (Queen Elizabeth Hall &
Schwetzingen Festival, Germany); Carmen
(Royal Opera House, Barcelona, Los Angeles
Opera & Washington Opera); Idomeneo,
(Welsh National Opera); I Due Foscari (Scottish
Opera); Cornet Rilke's Song of Love and Death
(Glyndebourne Opera); Queen of Spades
(English National Opera).

Barry Howard
Theatre includes: Twelfth Night, Julius Caesar
(Comedy); Salad Days, Oliver, Boys in the Band,
Fiddlers Five, Bedful of Foreigners, One for the
Pot, The Pirates of Penzance, The Rocky
Horror Show (tour); Cabaret (Bristol Old Vic);
Run for Your Wife (Critereon); Hi-De-Hi!
(Summer Season and Victoria Palace); Winnie
(Victoria Palace); Don't Dress For Dinner, Out
of Order, Bedfull of Foreigners, His Favourite
Family, What A Racket (Summer Season). Over
forty pantomimes best forgotten.
Television includes: Hi-Di-Hi, The House of
Windsor, Dad, You Rang M'Lord, The Two
Ronnies, Kelly Montieth Show, Terry and June,
3-2-1.

Rob Howell (designer)
For the Royal Court: Real Classy Affair, Simpatico.
Other theatre includes: Snow Orchid, Salvation (Gate); Relative Values (Chichester Festival /Savoy /Tour); Eurovision (Sydmonton Festival & Vaudeville); Oliver! (Crucible, Sheffield); Private Lives (Dalateatern, Sweden); Julius Caesar (Royal Exchange, Manchester); True West (West Yorkshire Playhouse/Donmar Warehouse); The Loves of Cass Maguire (Druid Theatre Company); Tartuffe, The Government Inspector (Almeida); Habeas Corpus, The Glass Menagerie, The Fix, How I Learned to Drive (Donmar Warehouse); Tom and Clem (Aldwych); Eddie Izzard – Glorious (Pola Jones); The Shakespeare Revue, The Painter of Dishonour, Little Eyolf, Richard III, Family Reunion (RSC); Chips With Everything, Troilus and Cressida, Money, Battle Royal (RNT); Entertaining Mr Sloane (Theatre Clwyd); Little Malcolm and His Struggle against the Eunuchs (Hampstead Theatre/West End); Vassa (Almeida at the Albery); Eddie Izzard (UK tour 1999/2000), Betrayal (Theatre d'Atelier, Paris). Awards include: Best Set and Costume Design, Olivier Awards 1999 for Battle Royal (RNT); nomination for for Best Set Designer, Olivier Awards 1997 for Chips With Everything (RNT); Olivier Award for Best Set Designer 1996 for The Glass Menagerie (Donmar Warehouse /Comedy Theatre); nomination for TMA Best Designer 1996 for Peter Pan (West Yorkshire Playhouse).

James Macdonald (director)
Associate director of the Royal Court since 1992.
For the Royal Court : Real Classy Affair, Cleansed, Bailegangaire, Harry and Me, The Changing Room, Simpatico, Blasted, Peaches, Thyestes, The Terrible Voice of Satan, Hammett's Apprentice.
Other theatre includes: The Triumph of Love (Almeida); Roberto Zucco (RSC); Love's Labours Lost, Richard II (Manchester Royal Exchange); The Rivals (Nottingham Playhouse); The Crackwalker (Gate); The Seagull (Sheffield Crucible); Neon Gravy (RNT Studio); Miss Julie (Oldham Coliseum); Juno and the Paycock, Ice Cream & Hot Fudge, Romeo and Juliet, Fool for Love and Savage/Love, Master Harold and the Boys (Contact Theatre); Prem (BAC, Soho Poly). Opera includes: Wolf Club Village, Night Banquet (Almeida Opera); Oedipus Rex, Survivor from Warsaw (Royal Exchange/Halle); Lives of the Great Poisoners (Second Stride).

Geoff Thompson (fight choreographer)
Qualifications include: 5th Dan black belt in Japanese Karate, 1st Dan in Judo, 3rd Dan in Jui-Jitsu. Senior Instructor level in many other forms of wrestling and martial arts.
Instruction includes: Chuck Norris UFAF Contributing Editor to Men's Fitness Magazine, Self Defence Columnist for Front Magazine. Published articles include: GQ, FHM, Maxim, Arena, Front, Loaded.
Books include: Watch My Back, Bouncer, On The Door.

Nicholas Woodeson
For the Royal Court: Bazaar, The Editing Process, Berlin Bertie, Doing the Business.
Other theatre includes: Art (Wyndham's); The Late Middle Classes (Watford and tour); Chimps (Hampstead Theatre); American Buffalo (Young Vic); Habeas Corpus (Donmar Warehouse); An Inspector Calls (West End/Broadway); The Birthday Party (RNT); The Homecoming (Comedy Theatre); The Possibilities (Almeida); The Art of Success (Manhattan Theatre Club); King John, Sarcophagus, Flight, Macbeth, A Midsummer Night's Dream, Crimes in Hot Countries, Red Noses, The Party, The Desert Air, Henry V, Good (RSC); Piaf (Broadway); Man and Superman (Broadway).
Television includes: Mrs Bradley's Mysteries, Great Expectations, Woman in White, The Last Englishman, Pie in the Sky, Men of the Month, The Chief, Cracker, Hedda Gabler, Mr Wroe's Virgins, Bonjour La Classe, The Life and Times of Henry Pratt, Bad Girl, Blackheath Poisonings, A Fatal Inversion, The Wolvis Family, For the Greater Good, Blackeyes, My Kingdom for a Horse, Miami Vice, The Hound of the Baskervilles, Here's Boomer, A Rumour of War. Film includes: Mad Cows, Topsy Turvy, Titanic Town, Dreaming of Joseph Lees, The Avengers, The Man Who Knew Too Little, Shooting Fish, The Pelican Brief, Maria's Child, The Russia House, Max and Helen, Heaven's Gate. Radio/Recording includes: The Merry Wives of Windsor, Plain Murder, Last Orders, Dreaming Up Laura.

THE ENGLISH STAGE COMPANY AT THE ROYAL COURT

The English Stage Company at the Royal Court opened in 1956 as a subsidised theatre producing new British plays, international plays and some classical revivals.

The first artistic director George Devine aimed to create a writers' theatre, 'a place where the dramatist is acknowledged as the fundamental creative force in the theatre and where the play is more important than the actors, the director, the designer'. The urgent need was to find a contemporary style in which the play, the acting, direction and design are all combined. He believed that 'the battle will be a long one to continue to create the right conditions for writers to work in'.

Devine aimed to discover 'hard-hitting, uncompromising writers whose plays are stimulating, provocative and exciting'. The Royal Court production of John Osborne's Look Back in Anger in May 1956 is now seen as the decisive starting point of modern British drama, and the policy created a new generation of British playwrights. The first wave included John Osborne, Arnold Wesker, John Arden, Ann Jellicoe, N F Simpson and Edward Bond. Early seasons included new international plays by Bertolt Brecht, Eugène Ionesco, Samuel Beckett, Jean-Paul Sartre and Marguerite Duras.

The theatre started with the 400-seat proscenium arch Theatre Downstairs, and then in 1969 opened a second theatre, the 60-seat studio Theatre Upstairs. Productions in the Theatre Upstairs have transferred to the West End, such as Conor McPherson's The Weir, Kevin Elyot's My Night With Reg and Ariel Dorfman's Death and the Maiden. The Royal Court also co-produces plays which have transferred to the West End or toured internationally, such as Sebastian Barry's The Steward of Christendom and Mark Ravenhill's Shopping and Fucking (with Out of Joint), Martin McDonagh's The Beauty Queen Of Leenane (with Druid Theatre Company), Ayub Khan-Din's East is East (with Tamasha Theatre Company, and now a feature film).

Since 1994 the Royal Court's artistic policy has again been vigorously directed to finding a new generation of playwrights. The writers include Joe Penhall, Rebecca Prichard, Michael Wynne, Nick Grosso, Judy Upton, Meredith Oakes, Sarah Kane, Anthony Neilson, Judith Johnson, James Stock, Jez Butterworth, Simon Block, Martin McDonagh, Mark Ravenhill, Ayub Khan-Din, Tamantha Hammerschlag, Jess Walters, Conor McPherson, Simon Stephens, Richard Bean, Roy Williams, Gary Mitchell, Mick Mahoney, Rebecca Gilman, Christopher Shinn and Kia Corthron. This expanded programme of new plays has been made possible through the support of the Jerwood Foundation, and many in association with the Royal National Theatre Studio.

In recent years there have been record-breaking productions at the box office, with capacity houses for Jez Butterworth's Mojo, Sebastian Barry's The Steward of Christendom, Martin McDonagh's The Beauty Queen of Leenane, Ayub Khan-Din's East is East, Eugène Ionesco's The Chairs and Conor McPherson's The Weir, which transferred to the West End in October 1998 and is now running at the Duke of York's Theatre.

The newly refurbished theatre in Sloane Square opened in February 2000, with a policy still inspired by the first artistic director George Devine. The Royal Court is an international theatre for new plays and new playwrights, and the work shapes contemporary drama in Britain and overseas.

REBUILDING THE ROYAL COURT

In 1995, the Royal Court was awarded a National Lottery grant through the Arts Council of England, to pay for three quarters of a £26m project to rebuild completely our 100-year old home. The rules of the award required the Royal Court to raise £7.5m in partnership funding. The building has been completed thanks to the generous support of those listed below. We are particularly grateful for the contributions of over 5,700 audience members.

If you would like to support the ongoing work of the Royal Court please contact the Development Department on 020 7565 5000.

ROYAL COURT
DEVELOPMENT BOARD
Elisabeth Murdoch (Chair)
Jonathan Cameron (Vice Chair)
Timothy Burrill
Anthony Burton
Jonathan Caplan QC
Monica Gerard-Sharp
Joyce Hytner
Dany Khosrovani
Feona McEwan
Michael Potter
Sue Stapely
Charlotte Watcyn Lewis

PRINCIPAL DONOR
Jerwood Foundation

WRITERS CIRCLE
BSkyB Ltd
The Cadogan Estate
Carillon/Schal
News International plc
Pathé
The Eva and Hans K Rausing Trust
The Rayne Foundation
Garfield Weston Foundation

DIRECTORS CIRCLE
The Esmée Fairbairn Charitable Trust
The Granada Group plc

ACTORS CIRCLE
Ronald Cohen & Sharon Harel-Cohen
Quercus Charitable Trust
The Basil Samuel Charitable Trust
The Trusthouse Charitable Foundation
The Woodward Charitable Trust

SPECIFIC DONATIONS
The Foundation for Sport and the Arts for Stage System
John Lewis Partnership plc for Balcony
City Parochial Foundation for Infra Red Induction Loops and Toilets for Disabled Patrons
RSA Art for Architecture Award Scheme for Antoni Malinowski Wall Painting

STAGE HANDS CIRCLE
Anonymous
Miss P Abel Smith
The Arthur Andersen Foundation
Associated Newspapers Ltd
The Honorable M L Astor Charitable Trust
Rosalind Bax
Character Masonry Services Ltd
Elizabeth Corob
Toby Costin
Double O Charity
The D'Oyly Carte Charitable Trust
Thomas and Simone Fenton
Lindy Fletcher
Michael Frayn
Mr R Hopkins
Roger Jospe
William Keeling
Lex Service plc
Miss A Lind-Smith
The Mactaggart Third Fund
Fiona McCall
Mrs Nicola McFarland
Mr J Mills
The Monument Trust
Jimmy Mulville and Denise O'Donoghue
David Murby
Michael Orr
William Poeton CBE and Barbara Poeton
Angela Pullen
Mr and Mrs JA Pye's Charitable Settlement
Ruth and Richard Rogers
Ann Scurfield
Ricky Shuttleworth
Brian Smith
The Spotlight
Mr N Trimble
Lionel Wigram Memorial Trust
Madeline Wilks
Richard Wilson
Mrs Katherine Yates

PROGRAMME SUPPORTERS

The Royal Court (English Stage Company Ltd) receives its principal funding from the London Arts Board. It is also supported financially by a wide range of private companies and public bodies and earns the remainder of its income from the box office and its own trading activities. The Royal Borough of Kensington & Chelsea gives an annual grant to the Royal Court Young Writers' Programme and the London Boroughs Grants Committee provides project funding for a number of play development initiatives.

Royal Court Registered Charity number 231242.

This year the Jerwood Charitable Foundation continues to support new plays by new playwrights with the fifth series of Jerwood New Playwrights. Since 1993 the A.S.K. Theater Projects of Los Angeles has funded a Playwrights' Programme at the theatre. Bloomberg Mondays, a continuation of the Royal Court's reduced price ticket scheme, is supported by Bloomberg News. BSkyB have also generously committed to a two-year sponsorship of the Royal Court Young Writers' Festival. Other People is supported by The American Friends of the Royal Court Theatre and Francis Finlay.

TRUSTS AND FOUNDATIONS
American Friends of the Royal Court Theatre
Jerwood Charitable Foundation
Laura Pels Foundation
The Peggy Ramsay Foundation
The John Lyons Charity
The Alan & Babette Sainsbury Charitable Fund
The John Studzinski Foundation
The Bulldog Princep Theatrical Fund
The Trusthouse Charitable Foundation

MAJOR SPONSORS
Marks and Spencer
Barclays Bank plc
Bloomberg News
BSkyB
Francis Finlay
Virgin Atlantic

BUSINESS MEMBERS
Agnès B
Cartier
Channel Four Television
Davis Polk & Wardwell
Goldman Sachs International
Laporte plc
Lazard Brothers & Co. Ltd
Lee and Pembertons
Mask
Mishcon de Reya Solicitors
Redwood Publishing plc
Simons Muirhead & Burton
Space NK
J Walter Thompson

INDIVIDUAL MEMBERS
Patrons
Advanpress
Associated Newspapers Ltd
Mrs Alan Campbell-Johnson
Gill Carrick
Citigate Dewe Rogerson Ltd
Conway van Gelder
Chris Corbin
David Day
Greg Dyke
Ralph A Fields
Mike Frain
Judy & Frank Grace
Homevale Ltd
JHJ and SF Lewis
Lex Service plc
Barbara Minto
New Penny Productions Ltd
Martin Newson
AT Poeton & Son Ltd.
Greville Poke
David Rowland
Sir George Russell
Mr & Mrs Anthony Weden
Richard Wilson
George & Moira Yip

Benefactors
Bill Andrewes
Batia Asher
Elaine Mitchell Attias
Jeremy Bond
Katie Bradford
Julian Brookstone
Yuen-Wei Chew
Carole & Neville Conrad
Coppard and Co.
Curtis Brown Ltd
Robyn Durie
Winston Fletcher
Claire & William Frankel
Nicholas A Fraser
Robert Freeman
Norman Gerard
Henny Gestetner OBE
Carolyn Goldbart
Sally Greene
Angela Heylin
Juliet Horsman
Amanda Howard Associates
ICM Ltd
Trevor Ingman
IPA
Lisa C Irwin
Peter Jones
Paul Kaju & Jane Peterson
Catherine Be Kemeny
Thomas & Nancy Kemeny
KPMG
CA Leng
Lady Lever
Colette & Peter Levy
Mae Modiano
Pat Morton
Joan Moynihan
Paul Oppenheimer
Mr & Mrs Michael Orr
Sir Eric Parker
Carol Rayman
Angharad Rees
John & Rosemarie Reynolds
John Ritchie
John Sandoe (Books) Ltd
Nicholas Selmes
Peregrine Simon
David & Patricia Smalley
Max Stafford-Clark
Sue Stapely
Ann Marie Starr
Charlotte Watcyn Lewis

AMERICAN FRIENDS
Founders
Victoria & David Elenowitz
Francis Finlay
Monica Gerard-Sharp & Ali Wambold
Donald & Mia Martin Glickman
Carl Icahn & Gail Golden
Jeanne Hauswald
Mary Ellen Johnson & Richard Goeltz
Dany Khosrovani
Kay Koplovitz
Stephen Magowan
Monica Menell-Kinberg PhD
Benjamin Rauch & Margaret Scott
Rory Riggs
Robert Rosenkranz
Gerald Schoenfeld

Patrons
Miriam Bienstock
Arthur Bellinzoni
Robert L & Janice Billingsley
Harry Brown
Catherine G Curran
Leni Darrow
Michael & Linda Donovan
April Foley
Richard & Linda Gelfond
The Howard Gilman Foundation
Richard & Marcia Grand
Paul Hallingby
Herrick Theatre Foundation
Maurice & Jean R Jacobs
Sahra T Lese
Susan & Martin Lipton
Anne Locksley
William & Hilary Russell
Howard & Barbara Sloan
Margaret Jackson Smith
Mika Sterling
Arielle Tepper
The Thorne Foundation

Benefactors
Tom Armstrong
Mr & Mrs Mark Arnold
Elaine Attias
Denise & Matthew Chapman
Richard & Rosalind Edelman
Abe & Florence Elenowitz
Hiram & Barbara Gordon
Brian & Araceli Keelan
Jennifer CE Laing
Burt Lerner
Rudolph Rauch
Lawrence & Helen Remmel
Robert & Nancy Scully
Julie Talen

AWARDS FOR
THE ROYAL COURT

Ariel Dorfman's Death and the Maiden and John Guare's Six Degrees of Separation won the Olivier Award for Best Play in 1992 and 1993 respectively. Terry Johnson's Hysteria won the 1994 Olivier Award for Best Comedy, and also the Writers' Guild Award for Best West End Play. Kevin Elyot's My Night with Reg won the 1994 Writers' Guild Award for Best Fringe Play, the Evening Standard Award for Best Comedy, and the 1994 Olivier Award for Best Comedy. Joe Penhall was joint winner of the 1994 John Whiting Award for Some Voices. Sebastian Barry won the 1995 Writers' Guild Award for Best Fringe Play, the 1995 Critics' Circle Award and the 1997 Christopher Ewart-Biggs Literary Prize for The Steward of Christendom, and the 1995 Lloyds Private Banking Playwright of the Year Award. Jez Butterworth won the 1995 George Devine Award for Most Promising Playwright, the 1995 Writers' Guild New Writer of the Year Award, the Evening Standard Award for Most Promising Playwright and the 1995 Olivier Award for Best Comedy for Mojo. Phyllis Nagy won the 1995 Writers' Guild Award for Best Regional Play for Disappeared.

The Royal Court was the overall winner of the 1995 Prudential Award for the Arts for creativity, excellence, innovation and accessibility. The Royal Court Theatre Upstairs won the 1995 Peter Brook Empty Space Award for innovation and excellence in theatre.

Michael Wynne won the 1996 Meyer-Whitworth Award for The Knocky. Martin McDonagh won the 1996 George Devine Award, the 1996 Writers' Guild Best Fringe Play Award, the 1996 Critics' Circle Award and the 1996 Evening Standard Award for Most Promising Playwright for The Beauty Queen of Leenane. Marina Carr won the 19th Susan Smith Blackburn Prize (1996/7) for Portia Coughlan. Conor McPherson won the 1997 George Devine Award, the 1997 Critics' Circle Award and the 1997 Evening Standard Award for Most Promising Playwright for The Weir. Ayub Khan-Din won the 1997 Writers' Guild Award for Best West End Play, the 1997 Writers' Guild New Writer of the Year Award and the 1996 John Whiting Award for East is East. Anthony Neilson won the 1997 Writers' Guild Award for Best Fringe Play for The Censor.

At the 1998 Tony Awards, Martin McDonagh's The Beauty Queen of Leenane (co-production with Druid Theatre Company) won four awards including Garry Hynes for Best Director and was nominated for a further two. Eugene Ionesco's The Chairs (co-production with Theatre de

Complicite) was nominated for six Tony awards. David Hare won the 1998 Time Out Live Award for Outstanding Achievement for Via Dolorosa. Sarah Kane won the 1998 Arts Foundation Fellowship in Playwriting. Rebecca Prichard won the 1998 Critics' Circle Award for Most Promising Playwright for Yard Gal.

Conor McPherson won the 1999 Olivier Award for Best New Play for The Weir. The Royal Court won the 1999 ITI Award for Excellence in International Theatre. Sarah Kane's Cleansed was judged Best Foreign Language Play in 1999 by Theater Heute in Germany. Rebecca Gilman won the 1999 Evening Standard Award for Most Promising Playwright for The Glory of Living.

In 1999, the Royal Court won the European theatre prize New Theatrical Realities, presented at Taormina Arte in Sicily, for its efforts in recent years in discovering and producing the work of young British dramatists.

ROYAL COURT BOOKSHOP

The bookshop offers a wide range of playtexts, theatre books, screenplays and art-house videos with over 1,000 titles.

Located in the downstairs BAR AND FOOD area, the bookshop is open Monday to Saturday, daytimes and evenings.

Many of the Royal Court Theatre playtexts are available for just £2 including the plays in the current season and recent works by Conor McPherson, Martin Crimp, Caryl Churchill, Sarah Kane, David Mamet, Phylis Nagy and Rebecca Prichard. We offer a 10% reduction to students on a range of titles.

Further information : 020 7565 5024

FOR THE ROYAL COURT

ARTISTIC

Artistic Director **Ian Rickson**
Director **Stephen Daldry**
Assistant to the Artistic Director **Jo Luke**
Associate Directors
Dominic Cooke
Elyse Dodgson
James Macdonald *
Max Stafford-Clark *
Richard Wilson*
Trainee Director **Dawn Walton****
Associate Director Casting **Lisa Makin**
Casting Assistant **Julia Horan**
Literary Manager **Graham Whybrow**
Literary Assistant **Daisy Heath**
Literary Associate **Stephen Jeffreys** *
Resident Dramatist **Simon Stephens** +
Voice Associate **Patsy Rodenburg**
International Administrator **Natalie Highwood**

YOUNG WRITERS' PROGRAMME

Associate Director **Ola Animashawun**
General Manager **Aoife Mannix**
Writers' Tutor **Nicola Baldwin**

PRODUCTION

Production Manager **Paul Handley**
Assistant Production Manager **Sue Bird**
Production Assistant **Rebecca Fifield**
Company Stage Manager **Cath Binks**
Head of Lighting **Johanna Town**
Deputy Electrician **Marion Mahon**
Assistant Electrician **Simon Lally**
Lighting Board Operator TD **Andrew Taylor**
Head of Stage **Martin Riley**
Stage Deputy **David Skelly**
Stage Chargehand **Eddie King**
Head of Sound **Paul Arditti**
Sound Deputy **Rich Walsh**
Sound Operator **Emma Laxton**
Head of Wardrobe **Iona Kenrick**
Wardrobe Deputy **Suzanne Duffy**
Maintenance Manager **Fran Mcelroy**

ENGLISH STAGE COMPANY

President **Greville Poke**
Vice Presidents **Jocelyn Herbert**
Joan Plowright CBE
Council
Chairman **Sir John Mortimer QC, CBE**
Vice-Chairman **Anthony Burton**
Members
Stuart Burge CBE
Martin Crimp
Judy Daish
Stephen Evans
Phyllida Lloyd
Baroness McIntosh
Sonia Melchett
James Midgley
Richard Pulford
Hugh Quarshie
Nicholas Wright
Alan Yentob

MANAGEMENT

Executive Director **Vikki Heywood**
Assistant to the Executive Director **Karen Curtis**
General Manager **Diane Borger**
Finance Director **Donna Munday**
Finance Officer **Rachel Harrison**
Re-development Finance Officer **Neville Ayres**

MARKETING

Head of Marketing **Stuart Buchanan**
Press Officer **Giselle Glasman**
Marketing Officer **Emily Smith**
Press Assistant **Claire Christou**
Box Office Manager **Neil Grutchfield**
Deputy Box Office Manager **Valli Dakshinamurthi**
Duty Box Office Manager **Glen Bowman**
Box Office Sales Operator **Carol Prichard,
Gregory Woodward**

DEVELOPMENT

Head of Development **Helen Salmon**
Development Associate **Susan Davenport** *
Appeals Officer **Sophie Hussey**
Administrative & Research Assistant **Olivia Hill**

RE-DEVELOPMENT

Project Manager **Tony Hudson***
Technical Director **Simon Harper**
Assistant to Project Manager **Monica McCormack**

FRONT OF HOUSE

Theatre Manager **Lucy Dusgate**
Deputy Theatre Manager **Jemma Davies**
Duty House Manager **Grainne Cook***
Bookshop Manager **Del Campbell**
Bookshop Assistant **Sarah Mclaren** *
Stage Door/Reception **Andrew Mcloglan, Tyrone
Lucas, Sophie Fox***, **Simon David***
Thanks to all of our ushers

* part-time
+ Arts Council Resident Dramatist
** recipient of a bursary from the Arts Council of England

Honorary Council
Sir Richard Eyre
Alan Grieve
Advisory Council
Diana Bliss
Tina Brown
Allan Davis
Elyse Dodgson
Robert Fox
Jocelyn Herbert
Michael Hoffman
Hanif Kureishi
Jane Rayne
Ruth Rogers
James L. Tanner

Hard Fruit

Characters

Choke
Sump
Mrs Kooee
Yack
Silver
Friar Jiggle
Two Men

Time
2000

Place
A small backyard of a terraced house, in a northern town

Note
This text went to press before the opening night and may therefore differ from the version as performed.

Act One

*Backyard of a terraced house. Lots of junk piled up the sides. Record player resting in junk pile, lead going up off into house, dusty old records piled beside it. Strange devices around the place, made from the junk, couple of them like figures made from springs and chair legs, etc. Sunrise over the backyard, the junk and the flagstones. A little elderly man (*Choke*) comes out into the yard. He is drinking from a massive cracked mug, the drink is steaming. In the pile of junk hangs a piece of tarpaulin. He finishes his drink. He goes towards the tarpaulin, reaches for it. Hears someone outside beyond the back wall, steps back. Suddenly a head appears above back wall. Big, bald (*Sump*).*

Sump Hey up.

Choke *nods.*

Gate opens, **Sump** *comes in, a big elderly man.*

Choke (*shouts*) Shut gate ahind ya!

Sump *turns and shuts back gate tight, latch rattles. He puts an old duffel bag down.*

Sump Mornin'.

Choke Mornin'.

They turn to each other and start fighting, wrestling, boxing, ju-jitsu. It's randori (*practice*). *Headlocks to armlocks, throws, chokes, strangles, grappling, groundwork. Furious. Fast.*

Then they stop for a breather.

Choke (*indicating duffel bag*) What you brought?

Sump Cornbeef doorsteps and some brondy snaps.

Choke Rubbish.

Sump So what.

They fight on.

They stop.

Choke *holding stomach.*

Choke   Aahh.

Sump   What's with you? I never went for t'beer bag.

Choke   You did!

Sump   I never.

Choke   You did, wi elbow, you sneaking swine!

Sump   Never noticed. Must be niftier than I thought, eh?

Goes for belly again with a mock low punch. **Choke** *turns away quick.*

They break.

Choke *still doubled over, he puts a brave face on it by turning it into collecting weeds and grasses from between the flagstones.*

Sump *goes and sits in the junk pile and starts going into his duffel bag for a sandwich. Big chunky doorsteps.*

Choke   Bit early for that.

Sump   Never too early for me.

Choke (*indicating something he can see inside open bag*)   What's them, books?

Sump   Library books. I'm taking them back after.

Choke   What are they?

Sump   Barbara Cartland.

Offering sandwich.

You want one?

Choke   No, I've had me drink.

Sump   Your drink? Stewed weeds from between the flagstones. What you doing now? What's that, your dinner there you're plucking?

Choke *nods.*

Sump (*mouthful*)   You wanna get yourself some food.

Choke   Sump.

Sump (*mouthful*)   Aye?

Choke   Button it.

Sump   You wanna get yourself some food. Get biting something. You need to chew, man, and swallow. Get your belly clunking, it needs something to squeeze on.

Choke *ignores him. He hangs picked weeds out to dry on record-player lead, which serves as a washing line as well.*

Sump   Why not get rid of some of this junk? Give us a bit more elbow room.

Choke   I need it.

Sump   Need it.

Choke *ignores him.*

Sump   What for? More contraptions that bloody fall to bits.

Sump *suddenly hits out at a training device nearby, it is shaped like a man made of springs and chair legs. His shot is sudden, fast and hard. The whole thing collapses in a cloud of rust.*

Choke   That was just in the making.

Sump (*laughs out loud*)   In the making. How come all your machines are just in the making?

Shaking his head.

Come on, have me last sandwich.

Holds out a massive white doorstep.

Choke *ignores him.*

Sump   They can help you grow, these, Choke. You don't need to eat 'em, just stand on 'em.

Sump *bites into the bread.*

Choke (*spinning round*)   What do you mean by that?

Sump (*munching*)   What?

Choke   You know.

Sump (*swallowing*)   Nothing.

Choke   Eh!

Sump   It was a joke about the sandwich.

Choke   Eh?

Sump   It was a joke about the sandwich.

Choke   Look at you, you great fat pig, look at you!

Sump (*nearly choking on his sandwich*)   Look at you!

Choke   Look at you!

Sump   Look at you! Anyway, at least I'm not weakening.

Choke   Weakening!

Sump   You know it, in the practice you're watery.

Choke   No.

Sump   You are.

Choke   No. Never. You're rubbish, you eat rubbish, you train rubbish.

Sump   Now now.

Choke   Look at you.

Sump   Don't start that again.

Choke   Look at you, you fat mountain.

Sump   Look at you, you short ar . . .

Choke(*meaning it*)   Don't say it or I'll kill you!

Sump   Short . . .

Suddenly a woman's head over wall next door.

Mrs Kooee   Koo eee.
Have you got a cup of sugar?

Sump   I know what you're after, come round.

Choke *tuts, turns away, tries to say something but too late.*

She comes round and through gate with an empty cup and a sleeveless record under her arm. Elderly woman in pinny.

Choke   Shut gate . . .

Mrs Kooee   . . . tight ahind you! I know, love.

Choke   Well, you should know I don't have sugar an' all.

Mrs Kooee   Oh, I forgot again

Sump   Give us the record, I'll put it on.

He goes to player.

Choke   The record player is for playing records that are for Indian club swinging only.

Sump   You say that every day.

Mrs Kooee   He does.

Sump   Yet every day we have our dance, don't we, Missus Kooee.

Mrs Kooee   We do, Mr Sump.

The music starts up off mono-portable, they dance all around yard, quite vigorously, rough-hewn but nice.

Choke *sits in corner sulking.*

The music stops.

Mrs Kooee   Thanks ever.

As she goes for the door she stops.

Choke.

He's not looking.

Sump   She's talking to you, Choke.

Choke *reluctantly turns to her.*

She quickly pulls out a pie from her pinny, offers it to **Choke**.

Mrs Kooee   Here's a pie.

Choke   You take it, I don't eat them.

Mrs Kooee   You used to.

Sump   Here, I'll have it, he used to do a lot of things. (*Taking it.*) Ta, Mrs Kooee.

Mrs Kooee (*to* **Choke**)   Never mind, there's something else warm and waiting for you whenever you want it.

Choke *grunts.*

Sump   OOOoooo.

Mrs Kooee (*laughing*)   Me here with two right bachelors.

Sump   Why don't you get him to go out with you sometime, Mrs Kooee?

Mrs Kooee   I keep trying to persuade him to come to Kwik Save with me. (*To* **Choke**.) Don't I?

Choke   Do you?

Sump   He's not been out for years. You couldn't keep him in at one time, you know. (*To* **Choke**.) Could ya, Choke?

Choke   I don't know.

Sump   When was the last time you went out?

Choke   I don't know. Look, are we training or what!

He starts clearing away the rusty pile of the collapsed device.

(*To* **Mrs Kooee**.)   Out!

She goes.

Choke   Shut that gate tight ahind ya!

She does. Latch rattles.

Sump *taking the silver-foil tray off the pie,* **Choke** *glaring at him.*

Suddenly **Mrs Kooee**'s *head comes over the next-door wall.*

Mrs Kooee   Chuck your undercrackers over any time, I'll rinse them through and throw them back.

Sump *laughs.*

Choke *scowls.*

Mrs Kooee *goes back down.*

Sump *bites into pie.*

Choke *walks off into his house.*

While he's gone, **Sump** *strolls about, finishing pie, looking at junk. He sees something on the floor, under the junk, he gets down to it, it's a letter all wet. He picks it up, lays it across his hands, reads it. Looks disturbed. Crouches down, puts it back. It has changed him.*

Choke *comes out looking more bad-tempered, yet somehow revived.*

Choke   Come on, anyway, let's get to it. You come here wasting the bloody morning. You want to train, let's train. No wonder you're lard.

Sump (*distracted*)   Eh?

Choke   I said come on. If you're gonna train, train. If you're gonna eat, become a pig.

He pushes him hard.

Sump *throws the last bit of pie at* **Choke** *with force.*

Choke *dodges it. He's fit now, on form, raring to go.*

They start in quite hard, then for some reason **Sump** *eases up a bit.*

Choke *stops.*

Choke   What's going on. You're too soft. What's up?

Sump   It's you.

Choke   Can't you hit?

Sump   I can hit all right.

Choke   Come on then.

They go in hard.

Then **Sump** *lets up.*

Choke   What is it?

Sump (*he can't say*)   I'm going.

Sump *picks up duffel bag on his way out.*

Choke (*casual*)   Aye, well, don't come back.

Sump   Eh?

Choke   I don't need you no more.

Sump *looks at him.*

Choke   I won't be needing you no more.

Sump   Eh?

Choke   I've been meaning to tell you for the last few weeks.

Sump *goes quiet as if expecting something very serious.*

Choke   I've something.

I've made myself . . .

Pause.

(*Not sure whether to say it, then does.*)   . . . a karate machine.

Sump *open-mouthed. Then starts laughing. Then stops.*

Sump   A what!

Choke   You heard.

Sump   Your . . . Oh, forget it, I'll see you tomorrow.

Choke (*shaking his head*)   No. I mean it. I don't need nothing or no one, no more.

Sump   Are you serious?

Choke *nods.*

Sump   You daft little get.

He wrestles the head of another training device and throws it at **Choke**. *He catches it.*

Sump   They fall apart.

Choke   This one don't.

Sump   You're falling apart.

Choke   I don't need you no more. How many more times.

Sump   You need all the help you can get from what I've seen.

He goes.

Choke   What do you mean by that?
Come back!

Rushes to open gate, can't go out, tries but somehow can't cross threshold.

(*Shouts.*)   Come back and finish what you're saying.

Mrs Kooee's *head comes over.*

Choke (*shouts after* **Sump**)   Go on then, get!

Mrs Kooee   But he's your old friend.

Choke   He's no friend, he was a ten-a-penny punchbag training partner. He doesn't know what training is, he doesn't know what a friend is. Keep your conk out, woman.

She pops back down.

He throws head of machine at her.

Suddenly sees gate still open.

Choke (*shouts*)   Shut gate tight ahind ya!!

Choke *slams gate.*

Latch rattles.

Rattles.

Stops.

Silence.

Choke *on his own.*

Looks lost, lonely.

Suddenly a high-pitched voice is heard.

Voice   Hey yoooouuu

He turns.

Voice   Over here, dummy.

He turns again.

It's a ginger cat on the back wall.

Cat   It's me, your conscience speaking.

Choke   Uh!

Cat   Why not come out? Come out here and play.

Choke   Eh?
I . . . Why are you talking?

Cat   Because I am. Come here, come out.

Choke   I . . . I don't know.

The cat is gone. Then the door opens and a thin elderly gay fellow steps in with the cat on his head, a little string pulls its mouth.

Yack   Hi, Choke, do you like me cat hat.

Choke *grunts.*

Yack *pulls the string, moves the mouth.*

Yack   Lovely, innit?

A good-looking cocky young gay comes in after him.

It's me cat hat, Gay Ginger . . . I made it from my
grandmother's stuffed cat. It's near enough all she left. Plus
a bowl of plastic fruit and a premium bond. I can remember
it when it was alive, hateful thing, it scratched my arse and
chased me backwards and made me sit on a jam sandwich.
A white slice on each shank and the jam between, the jam
between. I'm convinced that's what gave me the way with
me that I have to this day. Anyway, it makes a lovely hat,
don't you think, very Davy Crockett (*Takes it off.*) Last of the
Monicas. Now, how about you, long time no see.

Choke   Umm.

Yack   Will you teach him how to bop people?
He's been getting hassle.
Come on, come here, you. Don't be shy.

He brings young man forward.

Yack (*to* **Choke**)   This is Silver.
(*to* **Silver**). This is Choke . . .

Silver *doesn't even reach out a hand.*

Yack   . . . or 'Short wi'out the second', that's what he
always said. (*To* **Choke**.) Dint you? Someone would come
up and say 'All right Short a . . .' I won't say it. Or 'move it,
Short ar . . .' and he'd jump in with 'Say Short but not the
second' and they didn't, did they? So they called him 'Short
wi'out second'. Well, that seemed a big title for such a short
ar . . . oops, sorry, nearly. So they changed it to Short for
short. Then to Strangler 'cause he was master of the choke-
out. He'd wring necks like Squeezey bottles, just like flicking
off light switches. But there was already a Strangler, see, a
half-caste, half a loaf, half-arsed, half-cut, Efalump of a
fellah from Oldham. (*To* **Choke**.) Remember him?

Choke   No.

Yack   You remember Strangler.

Choke   I don't!

Yack   A sailor. Fingers like bananas. I called him Fumbler meself. A very boring man always on about his travels and figgy-bottomed Arabs. I was glad when he set sail again. Frilly Freddie got a card from him saying he'd had a terrible experience marooned alone at sea, probably bored himself daft, it was signed 'Admiral Dorothy'. Where was we, oh yeah, so (*Fast.*) 'Short wi'out second' then 'Short' then Strangler then 'Chokey' then 'Choke'. That's right, innit? It is. I'm glad we sorted that. What the fuck his real name was we'll never know. (*Gazing at* **Choke**.) I always thought there was something of the Cagney about him (*to* **Silver**), don't you, but smaller even, springier even. I'll tell you what, we was safe, in them days, no one would touch us 'cause of them, him and the other black belts. (Low to **Silver**.) Pink belts.

Choke   What?

Yack   I was saying you and the other judo blokes, tough, me and the other nancies used to call 'em the 'Hard Fruits'. They stood at the corner of the bar, and we moved in and out of 'em like butterflies. Big buggers most of 'em, with that V to 'em, cut like a wedge of cake, I loved that, I loved Steve Reeves, Mr Universe and Hercules, when he twisted his waist went that big. (*Shows with finger and thumb a ridiculously small width. Then indicating* **Short**.) Well (*Fast.*) 'Short wi'out second' 'Short' 'Strangler' 'Chokey choke' was the dinky model of them, if you will. But quick to take offence, he'd be on bar, or stool, arm round neck before they even knew it. A baby arm, around a man-size neck and they'd be out. Only seemed soft pressure, like hugging a pillow, but the purple-faced bastards fell, under pub tables they'd slither like a cartoon cat. You should a seen it.

Silver *looks bored stiff.*

Choke   Well, I admit I was the choke man, then as now.

Yack   You see. See, it's coming back to you now.
Remember the pub, the Hive?

Choke   No.

Yack   You do! A pub with a boxing gym upstairs. After
hours the landlord would put on his dress and let us all run
wild in the gym. Do you not remember, we'd all sing. (*Sings.*)
'Kiss me, Honey, Honey, Kiss me' all running round the
ring naked.

Choke   Not me. I was there but I didn't get in the ring.

Yack   Er . . . I don't know. (*Not sure but agrees.*) No, you
didn't.

Choke   I know I didn't.

Yack   You definitely didn't. No.

Choke   Anyway, you better go. Thought I'd seen the last
of you and your type. I've not seen you for years, what you
coming round for?

Yack   It's just Silver, like I said. He needs to know how to
protect himself proper.
Well, will you show him?
Zoom sent us.

Choke   Zoom.
Oh, all right then.
Zoom?

Yack   Yes.

Choke   Zoom dee doomdee or Polish Zoom?

Yack   Zoom dee doomdee.

Choke   I thought he was dead.

Yack   Well, he's large as life down the Star and Garter
Saturday afternoons. He bit a pool ball in half last week. He
must be one hundred years old but he's the same as ever.
(*Whispers to* **Silver**) A rough tough puff.

Choke   Eh?

Yack   Nowt. Nothing. Nowting.
So will you show him? If not for the olden days, for Zoom dee.

Choke   Er . . .

Silver   Hang on, I've had enough of this shite. (*Looking at* **Choke**.) Is this the Seven Samurai or the Seven Dwarfs?

Choke *suddenly drops him with a punch to a nerve centre.*

Yack   Oh God. (*To* **Choke**.) He's dreadful I know that, I know that but ohhhh. (*Cradling* **Silver***'s face.*)

Choke   I'll get him something.

Choke *goes off.*

Yack *helps* **Silver** *up and sitting.*

Yack   He's good, int he?

Silver *looks at him wide-eyed in disbelief that he could say that.*

Yack (*lowers his voice*)   He was always like that, him. Never let his guard down, never. He's one o' them like these minicab drivers, who meet in the Pig and Whistle, they won't admit they're gay. They just think they're blokes who just like a look at someone's bottom or knob. They never never never never come out 'cause they don't think there's 'owt to come 'owt of. Take my word, behind that crust there's a lovely little fairy waiting to fly free.

He looks around.

Oh, look, a record player.

Goes to it. Picks up old records. Reading labels.

'Marching bands'. 'Soldier tunes'. 'Regimental music for Callathenics'.
It's for exercises, like ancient Jane Fonda.
(*Looking.*) Has he no Burt Bacharach?

Head comes over next-door wall. It's **Mrs Kooee**.

Mrs Kooee   I have a record.

Yack   Ooh. (*Skips over to her.*) Sling it here dear.

She does, he catches it, puts it on.

Dances all over the yard, very good, like Fred Astaire, up the junk, off it, all over. **Mrs Kooee** *watches with glee. The lad laughing, through his pain.*

Choke *comes back in with a compress. Turns player off.*

Choke   Come on, none of that in my yard.

Yack   Okay, okay. Thanks, Missus . . .

Mrs Kooee *pops down quick.*

Yack (*to* **Silver**)   Are you staying?

Silver *nods.*

Yack *grabs up his cat hat, puts it on, but it's backward with the cat's arse facing out.*

Yack   Meet you later then, see you, 'Short wi'out second' 'Short' 'Strangler' 'Chokey choke'. See ya. (*Blows a kiss.*) Oops. (*Turns cat round the right way. In cat's voice, pulling string:*) See yaaaa.

He goes, dancing out.

Choke   Shut that gate tight ahind ya!

It bangs, rattling, shut.

Pause.

Suddenly **Yack** *pops up from behind wall, like on a trampoline.*

Yack   'Shut that door.'

Then he's gone again.

Silence.

Choke (*handing compress to* **Silver**)   Put this against your neck it'll stop any swelling.

Silver   I'm okay.

Choke   It'll do it.

Silver *shakes his head.*

Choke   Please yourself.

Throws it into bins. Wipes his hands.

Choke *says nothing but starts slowly circling* **Silver**, *looking at him.*

Silver *looks back. Then can't take his stare and looks away.*

Choke *keeps looking.*

Silver (*impatient*)   When . . .

Choke   Quiet. You listen from now on. You can question at the end. Maybe.

Circles some more, stops.

(*Half to himself, half to* **Silver**.)   The first man who taught me, was a quiet man, very skilled. Very strong. We trained hard in them days, I still prefer the fifties things. Chest expanders. (*He pulls out rusty ones from junk.*) Indian clubs to music. (*Gets a pair out, twizzes them around a bit.*) Medicine ball. (*Gets one up out of junk pile, looks light in his hands, throws it at* **Silver**. *He tries to catch it, it knocks him on the floor.*)

See it wasn't the sauna- and gym-type of health they have now, we was after hard insides, like tyres, tubes and pipes. Hard outsides that could take a knock. Teacher Walt trained with his own things, made 'em. Paint tins full of cement, an axle from a car, plant pots full of gravel, carried 'em with his fingers like that. (*Makes a claw.*) Like that, up and down the back street in the moonlight, like that. No pain would make him let go. Many a night when he'd gone, I'd see a trail of his blood, trickling through the cobbles like cut knuckles.

Once a year he used to cover himself completely in honey and malt. You couldn't break his skin. It was lino.

Pause.

He was nearly sixty when I met him, but I saw him once somersault over a table and land with a foot in a bully's balls. Such control of his body even at that age, his body was his completely. It did as it was told. In his ordinary clothes, mac and that, you'd think he was just an ordinary Lancashire beer and pigeon bloke, but underneath was a kind of flat-cap Samurai. Disciplined, always on guard, aware, in control.

He took me on because I was little and vulnerable. He was sharing the strength out, spreading the code. Honour. Deceny. If he caught us throwing our weight about, being too flash with it, he would have found us, hurt us, left a mark, so we would not forget our whole lives.

Bloody hell he was fast. Bloody hell he was powerful, when he hit somebody it was like they'd been dumped off a truck, one strike, no follow-up needed, there they were covered in claret kissing kerb.

Silver *looks uncomfortable.*

Choke   What's all this to do with looking after yourself! Eh? Eh!

Silver *a bit scared.*

Choke   Teacher Walt's last fight was with a man in a bookies. I believe it was so full of smoke, you could only half see, it was like two dogs fighting in the fog. Two dragons in the mist. They was grappling, ripping, that wasn't his way, he didn't like mess. He got some space with a shin kick, then struck him! It would look like a touch to you. His skill was very high. Just two fingers, between the upper lip and the nose and down the man went, same as ever, but this time it was different, the cheering went to a pindrop, the tellies went off, he'd put too much force in, next to nowt, but the difference was there between life and death. and the man died on the betting-shop floor. Maybe it was the smoke affected his distancing, the adrenalin of the crowd, his judgement, but he let go control. We hardly saw him after that. The teaching stopped. He went to drink. He never got over it. One slip of control, the lot went, bit by slip till he died in his overcoat under a railway bridge, an empty gin bottle in every pocket, a throat full of sick, a waster!

IT'S SERIOUS. Even a man like that can go too far, IT'S SERIOUS. Check, we must check ourselves. We must have control and respect.

He glares at **Silver**.

I tell you this to clean your mind for the lesson. For your mind must be clean when you learn it. And your life should be as clean as you can live it. Your toughest fight will be with yourself. So you listen now and move and follow everything I say. Follow me! exactly! doing what I say step by step. Total obedience, understand?

Silver *nods*.

Choke   Stand

Silver *does but slowly with a slouch*.

Choke   Right, if somebody comes at you. This is your space. (*Puts hands up in an open-handed guard*.) Don't let 'em in. If they step forward. (*Indicating to* **Silver**.) Come on. Slowly.

Silver *does*.

Choke *responds with a strike, slowed down*.

Choke   And again. Slow.

Silver *does*.

Choke *again shows technique slowed down*.

Choke   And again, nice and slow.

Silver *suddenly does it really fast.*

Choke *responds faster, putting him down.*

Silver *squeals out in pain.* **Choke** *stands over him panting with anger.*

Silver   Fuck you. I only want it to fight off the punters and drug dealers if they get heavy!

Choke (*can hardly speak*)   Get up.

Silver *looks at him fearful that if he gets up he'll hurt him again.*

Choke   Get up!

Silver, *slowly and afraid, does, holding himself.*

Choke   Now get out.

Silver *heads for gate.* **Choke** *turns away in disgust.*

As he's not looking, **Silver** *suddenly hits him one below in side of stomach.*

Choke *goes down.*

Silver *stands over him.*

Silver *sees he's really hurt. Seems more than just ordinary reaction. Frightens* **Silver**, *he goes to try and help him up.*

Choke   No no, I should a seen it coming. Don't touch me!

He crawls towards his house.

Mrs Kooee's *head comes over next-door wall.*

Mrs Kooee   Oh my God, I'll phone for an ambulance.

Choke   No! No! Don't dare phone anyone. Leave me!

He crawls towards his house.

Blackout.
Lights up. Backyard. Back gate wide open. This empty set held for quite a time.

Then **Sump** *comes in through gate. Surprised to see it's open. Looks in and around, enters. He goes off to house, calls.*

Sump   Choke.

Comes back into yard perplexed.

He goes to an apparatus dummy standing off wall on springs. He wrestles with it a bit, it makes a noise, comes apart, he throws it on rubble.

Mrs Kooee *pops head over.*

Mrs Kooee   Koo ee.

Sump   Where's Choke? He can't be out, can he?

Mrs Kooee   I wunt know, Mr Sump. I've had the twin-tub on, it's like a combine harvester and Jimmy Young on top o' that. I can't hear a thing. All I know is he doesn't go out. He won't be out in my opinion.

Sump   No.

Mrs Kooee   Maybe he's in bed on the couch.

Sump   Choke!

Mrs Kooee   He were hurt pretty bad earlier, you know.

Sump   No, I didn't know.

Mrs Kooee   Some young brigand dealt him a dirty un, below stairs. I thought he was going to die. He couldn't get up.

Sump   That's not Choke, he never goes down.

Mrs Kooee   I know. I know.
I tell you I've got the worries about him. My nerves are in the wind with the washing, about him, I tell you. He's just nowhere near himself.

Sump *nods.*

Sump   He's saying and doing a lot of funny things lately, that's for sure.

Mrs Kooee   And with him you can't put it down to the drink.

Sump   Has he said about karate machine?

Mrs Kooee   I've heard him say it.

Sump   What's it spose to be?

Mrs Kooee   I don't know. I've only heard him say it in a sort of blether.

Sump   Is it in his head?

Mrs Kooee   I've never seen it. That's what I mean, it's like feverish talk.

Suddenly a big frightening noise.

Sump   What the hell's that!

Mrs Kooee   That's me twin-tub, second rinse.

She's gone.

Sump *goes towards* **Choke**'s *house and off.*

Set empty. **Choke** *enters, holding himself, panting. A brick in his hand. He goes in and behind open gate.*

Sump *returns. Doesn't see* **Choke** *behind open gate.*

Sits in pile.

Suddenly gate slams shut with a rattling latch.

Sump *jumps.*

Chok (*gone a bit hysterical*)   They're coming with their half bricks, I know they are.

Sump   What you on about? Where you been? You never go out!

Choke   I had to. Someone stole it.

Sump   What?

Choke   My karate machine!

Sump What you on about?

Choke I TOLD YOU! I told you! My karate machine! My karate machine! I built a karate machine! A karate machine for my old age.

Sump Okay. Okay, who's supposed to have taken it?

Choke How do I know! I don't know. That's why I went out. I got as far as the backs and they started. Lads, saying things, throwing a brick, I could have . . . I caught it with my bare hands. They'd gone. It was the name.

Sump What?

Choke You know it. It's not in the Bible.

Sump Eh?

Choke I knew I shouldn't a gone outside, they'd forgotten all about me. (*Suddenly desperate.*) What am I going to do!

He walks forward with brick, puts it down and slices it in two with a chop.

What I could a done to them.

Sump Look, calm down, Choke, go in and lie on the couch. Have a cup o' one of your teas.

Choke It's your fault too.

Sump Me!

Choke Yes, coming here, they know you and what you do and that tars me.

Sump Tars you!

Choke Dirties me name.

Sump What name?

Choke You wouldn't understand.

Sump I understand all right, you're losing it.

Choke   I can kill. I could have killed you. I had my karate machine. Someone's had it.

Sump   Or was it ever there?

Choke   Don't start that.

Sump   Choke . . . (*Going towards him.*)

Choke   Keep away.

Sump   I want to help you.

Choke   Keep away, Filth!

Sump (*losing his temper now*)   Fruitcake.

Choke   Hog.

Sump   Fool.

Choke   Scum.

Sump   Loon.

Choke   Lump.

Sump   Short ar . . .

Choke   I'll kill you.

Suddenly gate opens. A really big man, fat, big face, flat nose, everything, a monster, steps in.

Man   Hello.
Hope I'm not inconvenient.

(*To* **Choke**.)   Hello, Sump said . . .

Choke   What's this.

Sump   Oh yeah, I forgot.

Man   Hello.
(*Reaching out his hand to* **Choke**.) I'm Friar Jiggle.

Choke (*flabbergasted*)   What is this! What's happening.
(*Head in hands. Then suddenly:*) Have you got my karate machine?

Friar Jiggle *looks at him confused.*

Friar Jiggle   Sump said . . .

Sump   I said for him to call round. It was ages ago. I was drunk.

Choke   What is this? (*Head in hands again.*) Is he a friar?

Sump   No. He's a gay bouncer from the Goosey Gander.

Choke   Oh, I see, Well, that explains it. Pity I need some praying. Some hard prayer. What's happening? Where am I? Why is there a puff friar in my yard.

Sump   Why do they call you friar, Friar?

Friar Jiggle   Friar reasons are fhree . . .

Choke   I don't want to know. What's happening to me?

Sump   It's just er the club's having a new window and he's painting it. Stained-glass-style a thing. He's trying to depict the gay history of the neighbourhood. He was saying how we was Founding Fathers, which we was like, in a way, pansy pioneers so to speak, in a way. I was flattered. I was drunk. I said he could do me and perhaps . . . perhaps you. I . . .

Choke   Arrrrrgh! . . . I'm . . . I . . . Get out. Get out! . . . I'm not. I don't. Get out. Get out.

Friar Jiggle   I'll be quick (*Pulls out a big pastry tube.*) Sump said . . . (*Reveals a pane of glass covered with velvet.*)

Choke   Out or I'll smash everything. Every brick, every bone I see. Is that glass! (*Indicating the square covered with velvet.*)

Friar Jiggle *moves it quick.*

Sump   Forget it for now, Friar, fuck off.

Friar Jiggle *gets going through gate.*

Mrs Kooee *comes up.*

Mrs Kooee (*to* **Friar Jiggle**)   Maybe later.

Pops down. **Choke** *spins round.*

Choke   SHUT GATE AHIND, AHIND. AHIND YA!
(*To* **Sump**.) That's what I mean. You flaunt yourself.

Sump   I know myself.

Choke   You don't live right!

Sump   You don't live at all.

Choke   You don't train proper!!

Sump   You train too much. It's a routine.

Choke   You eat rubbish!

Sump   I enjoy my food.
(*Sings*.) 'Let's call the whole thing off.'

Choke   Take me serious! Take me serious!

Sump   You take everything too serious.

Choke   You do what you want. You take nothing serious,
you, your life's everywhere.

Sump   You're stuck to your routines and they're stuck to
you. You can't move.

Choke   You eat . . .

Sump   Rubbish! I know. How can it be? Grub I lub, all
types, and it lubs me. It's all health food to me. I don't think
you've enjoyed a mouthful for years. Even in the old days
when you ate half proper, you used to peel chips.

Choke   Eh!

Sump   You know you did, pat off the grease then peel a
perfectly good chip before nibbling it.

Choke   Shut up. I don't know! If so, it was for the
training. Something you'll never know.

Sump   No, you're right. Training's just something I do
'cause I do. Training's just . . . I don't know what . . .

Choke   I'll tell you what! It's a bloody hobby to you, to me it's life.

Sump   Aye, training every minute of the day for an attack that might never happen.

Choke   Shut up and go and have sex, that's your life.

Sump   Not all, my dear, but I do have my ports of call.

Choke   Disgusting at your age.

Sump   Disgusting at your age you don't.

Choke   It's the way . . .

Sump   So I like a sex-wrestle with men. So what! I'll tell anyone.

Choke   I know you will, I know! And it's not just . . .

Sump   Men, go on say it.

Choke (*quiet*)   It's not just men.

Sump   Well, I admits it has happened with women, I won't say no, in a lovey-dovey, soft, slip in, sort of way. From both being drunk on a bed or couch, a one-round knock-off. But with me big buckarooing blokes, it's a dirty free-for-all. Oh, I enjoy a fiddle a bumble a poker a tup. I'd a made a good Dickensian puff, I like ducking under dirty washing into hidey-holes. My sex drive's still flushing through, thank God. Where's yours? Jammed by a rusty stop tap at the end of your pipe, nowt up it but a clinging drip.
What a waste.

Choke   You're the waster. You fritter away every day.

Sump   Maybe I do.

Choke   You do! Come on, what do you do of a day that's worth anything, 'cept come here?

Sump   Let's see. Of a morning I get up, have a warm
drink in front of the fire. What do you do? You put your
head in a bucket of cold water and run round the yard.

Choke   We're not talking about me.

Sump   I look in the mirror. I'm pleased with meself, I've
got what I always wanted in old age, a figure like a
strongman from the *Dandy*. I rarely get ill, it feels like me
stomach's got a lining of greaseproof paper and all me veins
is done with Vim. I go out. Have a read and a chat down
the library by the warm pipes. Have a walk through the
park about ten miles per flower. I buy meself a cassette or
LP from the charity shop every week, sometimes it's a good
un like Boy George and I make up a dance in the kitchen. I
sometimes pop in the Lesbian café where they shave my
head for me and give me a hot pot, else a slap-up curry from
Paki Miranda. I'll take a pint at night or go round
someone's, or someone might come round or I'll sit in with
a warm milk wi a brondy in it. At weekends I'll go to a club
with the young uns. I just do what I want. What about you?

Choke *stands quiet.*

Sump   Sniff the flowers, you daft bastard, before it's too
late.

Choke *rocks a little in shock at this, then stands quiet.*

Sump   Well, what about you?

Choke   You know nothing.

Sump   I've seen it, Choke.
I've read the wet letter under there.

Choke   Eh?

Sump   You're ill, the doctors want you. You won't go,
you'll die if you don't.
Go, Choke.

Choke   I didn't need them. I had my karate machine.

Sump   Oh, not again.

Choke   Arrrrgh.
Why do you come here if you don't believe anything I say
or do?

Sump   I don't know. But I know you gotta let your guard
down at least now!

Choke   I don't need you. Fight me!

Sump   Let go, Choke, and live on the planet, admit you're
weak and lost like the rest of us. Let people help. Unclench
for once, little un. Let people in. You might die, for God's
sake.

Choke   Fight me. If you know so much. Come on!

Sump   No.

Choke   Fight.

Choke *goes for him.*

Sump *moves.*

Sump   I won't.

Choke   Fight me!

He starts to chase him.

FIGHT! Fight!

Sump   No!

Sump *moving back and around the yard.* **Choke** *after him.*

Choke   FIGHT.

Sump *slips out the gate.*

Choke *running round on his own with the momentum.*

Choke   FIGGHHHTTTT!

He falls on floor, rolling, then up.
He shouts out.

Shut door ahind ya! SHUT DOOR AHIND YA!

He shouts out.

Karate machine! Karate machine!

He puts record on of marching military band. Starts club-swirling to it. Loud old-fashioned marching music.

Karate machine! Karate machine!

Suddenly half bricks start coming over. They hit things. Hit him. Hit record player, needle screeches off record. He gathers some of the bricks up, dashes outside. Pauses at gate, then steps out of back gate throwing them. See him. Then see him retreat a bit in the shower of half bricks that keeps coming. Then go forward into it, shouting.

The set is empty. Hear in the distance, lads. Brick battling. Shouts.

Then silence.

He comes back in, covered in blood.

Picks up clubs, starts swirling them, singing 'Kiss me, Honey, Honey, Kiss me'. Smears blood over his mouth.

Choke   Is this to be my lipstick.

Carries on swinging and singing.

Act Two

Backyard. Night. Dark sky, stars up, moon. **Mrs Kooee** *is in yard, clearing away the blood, swishing it down with a bucket of water and a brush, washing it down like a slaughterhouse yard.* **Choke** *comes out in vest and braces, plasters on him, a bandage on his arm. Hair standing up everywhere, looking not there.*

Choke   I'll do that.

Mrs Kooee   No you don't, get back in.

Choke   I'll do it.

Mrs Kooee   Get back in and get your coat on.

Choke *goes in.*

She carries on finishing off, with a big-bucket swish.

He comes back out with a big mac on.

Mrs Kooee   Finished now.

Choke *takes brush and does last bit.*

She sits in pile.

He stops, holding brush like in pain, then distant.

Mrs Kooee   You all right?

Choke *sits down in pile too, nods.*

Mrs Kooee   Beautiful moon.

He doesn't even look up, just nods.

How are you?

Choke   Weakening. That's why I need the karate machine.

Mrs Kooee   What is it? Like these? (*Pointing to punch poles.*)

Choke   No. I know nobody believes me, I don't believe meself now. I know it might not be true. I think. Things keep slipping and dripping round me mind at times.

When I think back now it's, the thoughts is frothy like in milk, I'm in a fever, see, sweating, can't sleep, come down here in the middle of the night, in the yard, under the cool moon and I just chalk it out, once I start I can't stop, I'm chalking it all over the yard, the karate machine plan, chalking it out in detail, all over, right through till dawn, on the flagstones, till I finish it, and the flagstones slowly turning gold in the rising sun like warriors' shields lay down in rows with the plan all across 'em. And I know I can make it, and I feel safe, and I know I can still train even if I'm bedrid. Just hold on tight and it'll take your arm, chitty chitty bam bam, your arm gets faster then fast. It's all I've got to protect me. An old man these days needs to defend himself, an old man needs a karate machine!

I din need no one when I had the machine. Where's it gone, Mrs Kooee! Did you not see?

Mrs Kooee   As you say, Choke, it might not a been there, it might a been a thingy, a mirage.

Choke   Sometimes I think that, but then I'm sure I finished it. I'm sure I did. I'm sure it was there. I'm going mad, my brains conning me. Sometimes thoughts gets stuck like toffee papers on a wheel, going round and round, too slow at first, then so fast I can't tell what's what. I can't trust me body! I can't trust me brain! Is everything going? What am I to do?!

Mrs Kooee   You're ill, aren't you, Choke?

Choke   Nobody was ever ill in my family. Nobody. See, illness was looked on as a weakness in my family. Nobody was ill, my family was strong, my father . . . did you know him?

Mrs Kooee   No.

Choke   I'm surprised. My father never even had a cold
and the hair on his chest was tangerine right up to his death.
All my family was long-livers, usually died only 'cause they
were falling off bridges, hit by trucks, dropped down pits. I
think there was scorn on me and my mam 'cause I was slow
to grow then stopped. My father's family was famous for
their Health and Strength, all brothers. I had to prove me
even more. I felt like my dad wanted to kill me for being
small. He ignored me most days, I adored him in all ways. I
think it was his way, I think that it was his way, I'm sure I
know it was his way of toughening me, putting me on a
mountain in the storm of life to see if I survived. I did. It was
chilly and cold. I climbed that mountain. I took my body to
the best it could go. I took on all comers. I was the choke
man. Thanks, Dad. I've kept to the routines. (*Nearly in tears.*)

Picks up medicine ball.

When they told me I was ill, I couldn't believe it, I'd never
seen a doctor in my life. I won't go back. They've stopped
writing now and they know if they call round I'll twat them.

I wouldn't have gone because of the pain, I'll fight pain. It
was the blood. It was the blood that sent me, not the pain,
honest, Dad. I couldn't pretend it was jam in the sink, and
my wee was maroon, like Ribena before the water.

*He stands up and walks away squeezing the medicine ball into his
stomach. Obviously in pain.*

Mrs Kooee   Oh, Choke.

Choke *recovering himself. Then all right.*

Choke   It's not so bad today, sometimes, oh, sometimes I
go daft with the pain and I'm waving at ghosts then they
turn dark and crouching like Grecian wrestlers on an old
vase trapped behind glaze, grinning, then calling out
horrible things like 'Cut him from his arse to his prick, see
the blood bubble and flick!' and their breath's black as a
cassock and it's all over me and I'm out again in again out
again in again riding the pain like a searing jelly horse.

Nothing to steady meself on just more and more of it. If you push into it, it presses up somewhere else. I don't want to go near that pain again. No.

Looking at ball against his stomach.

It must be a medicine ball inside me by now. It was like a walnut they said when they first saw me. It's a coward, this illness, craven, cowering, advancing in the dark when no one's looking. Killing you behind your back. I have no self-defence for that type of attack. It might be a medicine ball inside me now, a rotting, meatball-and-blood malignant 'bad medicine' ball. Squashing my real organs into the wrong place, a swollen cuckoo in a blood nest.

Shouts to it.

Come out and fight! I'll take you on one cell at a time, step outside!

I'm weakening by the second. Whatever happened I always knew my bones was strong, now I can feel 'em going brittle and soft like Blackpool rock. I'm soft, I'm helpless, look at me blethering in front of you, the weakness I've always held off. I'm scared! While it swells I shrivel, my bones is Blackpool rock, brittle, white, with a streak o' pink. Is my blood pink! Does it slip through sissy insides that are like crumpled crushed velvet? Am I a girl?!

Mrs Kooee *puts her arm around him, sits him down.*

Mrs Kooee   Oh, Choke.

Choke *knocks her off. Then realises what he's done and is sorry.*

Choke   Sorry. Sorry. Sorry, I never hug. I never touch people, 'cept in a headlock or with a block. I don't know how to.

I'll tell you something now, I might as well, I'm the oldest living virgin.

Laughs. She laughs with him.

The nearest I got to sex with a woman was when someone fixed me up. He asked everyone to go out with me, they all said no, except Mog Duck, the scruffiest lass in the class. We ended up between some cars on a scrapyard, standing on shattered windscreen glass. She could sense my hesitation. She said if you don't want to go the whole hog just have finger pie. It knocked me right off, the wording, I don't know.

I found out that really all's I could ever do wi girlies was waltz a bit and make 'em laugh doing the eyebrow dance.

He does the eyebrow dance.

She laughs.

See what I mean, you do it, which moves the scalp, which I think sexies you, the female, up, which is why you laugh.

Mrs Kooee   You're so cute, you know, Chokey, so sort of innocent.

Choke (*not sure of this*)   Eh?

Mrs Kooee   I call you a secret name, do you want to know it?

Choke *half nods.*

Mrs Kooee   I call you 'Midget Gem'.
I'm sure a lot of woman have fallen for you from afar. The little loner, diddy but by God fanciable.

Choke   Oh no, it's not that I couldn't have them, that's not it, I knew I could a had 'em, I had the scalp and that, but I couldn't. I don't like the feel of 'em, everything gives, all pushy instead o' pressy, all wishy instead o' washy, all pie instead o' meat. No offence, Kooee.

Mrs Kooee   None tooked.

Pause.

Choke (*beginning to fret again*)   Where is it?

Mrs Kooee   What?

Choke   You know. The karate . . .

She touches his shoulder.

She takes her record out of her pinny, puts it on. They waltz.

It soothes him.

They waltz beautiful under the moonlight.

Then at back gate a knock.

They stop dancing.

It slowly opens.

Friar Jiggle *puts his big head round the door.*

Friar Jiggle   Hope I'm not inconvenient, lady and sir.

Choke *bristles.*

Mrs Kooee   Let him in, why not?

Choke *mellows again. Nods his head as though to say come in.*

Friar Jiggle *comes in. He has glass under velvet. He seems to have a funny accent, or might be he's a bit punchy or never learned to speak properly or pronounce his words.*

Friar Jiggle   Tank you. Tanky. I like paint you. On this pane. (*He removes cover.*) Then this pane go wid rest, make massive window. All pieces together.

He props it up.

Friar Jiggle *looking at* **Choke***, looking at glass.*

Choke (*stiffening a bit*)   You thinking you could have got me on a smaller piece than that?

Mrs Kooee *laughs to try and smooth things over.*

Friar Jiggle   No. No. I know you little but for capture your famous spirit I need glass of Crystal Palace, maybe more.

Choke *blushes at this but it melts him.*

Choke   Where do you want me?

Mrs Kooee *pats him on back and slips out.*

Friar Jiggle   Just there. Just there. No take long.

Friar Jiggle *quickly finds somethings to sit on and sits in front of glass. Pulls out a tube from his pocket.*

Choke *goes into a sort of old-fashioned strongman pose.*

Friar Jiggle   No take long. I quick be.

He starts going with pastry hose full of lead. Looking quick at **Choke** *then back at glass. We the audience can see it growing.*

Choke   So you're a bouncer?

Friar Jiggle   Yes I is.
I do not recommend violence but if I see a naked snoz I has to punce it.

He works on.

Choke   When did you start doing this?

Friar Jiggle *talks as he works.*

Friar Jiggle   When I was kid I did nothing but draw. No reada-writa, just draw.
If anyone disturb me, except my muder, Goid res' her, I punce em out. Kids, teacher even, punce.
Soon I'm passed from one place to another. Only thing same drawing, drawing. Puncing. Puncing.
Soon I get wid bad people. They want me punce for money.
Then I get wid my people, my parish and I home is.
I not draw for years then one night I help to decorate cake with Lil in kitchen at club. I make it really nice. Then instead of icing I use lead on a pint glass, nicer. Then on whisky glass wid colours, here I am.
I wan make windi nicest yet.
Tapestry-type thing.
All the peepoh who suffered for all the peepoh who now enjoy.

It big, everyone from streets can see it big in the wall, everybody must see it as they pass.

Pause as he works. **Choke** *still stock-still in position.*

Friar Jiggle   Your name, Choke?

Choke   Yeah.

Friar Jiggle   Why?

Choke   I was the choke man, knew all the chokes and strangles oriental and western. Still do. Practise them all every day.

Friar Jiggle   Aye, see, aye.

Pause.

Sump, why he dat name?

Choke   Because he used to flatten men with something between a slap and a thump.

Friar Jiggle   Aye, see, aye.

Choke   Why do they call you Friar?

Friar Jiggle   Frair reasons Fhree.
One. I worked as only bouncer at the Temple club.
Two. When I grab trouble-maker or sinners, I gid 'um three seconds to confession make before I knock 'em out.
Free. I oversee me parish.

Choke   Aye, see, aye.
Who's your parish?

Friar Jiggle   All the gay I meet. My parish is all puff. But once in, I protect you with punce and prayer. I am a shepherd to my frock.

Paints on, gets his coloured inks out now.

I did Yack other day, could not get his mouth be still long enough for finish it. You know Yack?

Choke   No.
Yes. Yess I do.
Yes.
I've got to stop this denying.

Friar Jiggle   Eh?

Choke   It's time to stop it.
Oh, but I've held it for so long.

Friar Jiggle *engrossed in work, not really listening. Then suddenly looks up.*

Friar Jiggle   I need it light more. Any more light?

Choke   Step on third flag to left.

Friar Jiggle *looks for it.*

Choke   It's connected from the outside lamp-post. I have it for night workouts.

Friar Jiggle *stamps on flagstone. Suddenly old car headlight in junk pile comes on bright, illuminating the wet flags, they shimmer and shine.* **Friar Jiggle** *sits again to work.* **Choke** *illuminated now like in a spotlight.* **Friar Jiggle** *in darkness now, working.*

Choke   Friar, I suppose you're the nearest I'll get to a priest. Friar, forgive me for I have sinned or is it for I have not sinned?

Pause.

I had a friend, we went everywhere together. He had everything, everything right. A real man. He was one of the physical culturists. He was big shouldered, neck, you know, back of his head brilliant with oil, blue suit, Sinatra-shiny or thin low-button cardigan, ever so thin chain. He could dress. You should a seen us, coming down back streets, round the corner, into a pub or café. Sometimes we worked out in the back room at his mam's she didn't mind, shoved the furniture back, moved the canary. We'd start with a hundred touch-toes. A hundred knee-bends. A hundred press-ups. That was just the warm-up. That was just the

warm-up, I'm telling you. There was sweat everywhere from
me, not from him. He had a springy quiv, it just sprung
there as he exercised. Once, we did a bit of catch as catch
can. I went down, him on top, he never crushed you
though, he was off like a cat. He started to describe to me
what you do to revive someone if you knock 'em out, kiss o'
life. As I listened to his description . . . there was in my
silence, summat . . . I don't know where it came from . . .
just . . . summat . . . and he stopped talking, and the quiet
went so deep there was no air, no one was breathing, I
thought the canary was going to die. Maybe that's when the
cell doubled up and the cancer first began to crawl.
He put his kit back on. I did. I went. We never spoke again.
After that if he came in a pub or a caff where I was, I had to
leave, I knew that, it was unspoken. Even though I knew he
never told anyone, I knew then that I would never be a real
man. (*Suddenly holding back tears.*) I had nearly bloody kissed
him.
But I never did it! Something rose in me that day but I
never let it out. Even so, I had to go me own way after that.
But, Friar, I must confess how I still cared for him, in fact
knowing I could never be near him again, the love cut
deeper. Samurai love, unspoken, carried for ever.
I found that you could stand with the men 'who had a way
with 'em' in the pub if you wanted, they was accepted, no
one bothered them, anyway they was big, like Rock
Hudson, a bigness soft-weighted. They looked after their
own. I'm talking about pubs wi' sawdust on the floor, I'm
talking about vaults, false teeth on the table, smoke holding
the place up, the beer in chunks. Hard places. And them
tender tough men at the bar end, near the Gents. Big judo
blokes some of 'em, always with half smiles and them
Hudson shoulders. But I couldn't join 'em, for a long time,
the three steps down the bar was too far, it was a hundred
mile. Then I can't remember how, but I did. Always round
the edge though, never going right in. If anybody saw they
could never quite say if I was with them or not. But as far as
they was concerned I was one of their own. You might just

still see that type today, older, grey, they wouldn't be able to stand the word gay. You might see 'em in a Berni Inn, Sunday cardigans on, four men having a meal, signet rings, good heads of hair. They're dying out together, that breed, end of an era.

Pause.

Friar, I haven't been out since age started on me, they might talk about me and what could I do. I'm at their mercy now, people know I never married, now I'm weakening they'll feel safe putting two and two together. But I never did it! Summat rose in me that day in his mam's back room but I've never let it out, no way! Shame and me with all our strength we've held it tight, it's in with the disease, they're both resting in the same spot. Can letting one out let out the other?
I never did it, Friar.
But I wanted to.

Long pause.

I keep dreaming of him lately, he's as in youth, he's radiant in a perfect white judo gi. I'm so glad to see him, I can't help myself and try to hold him but the white light of his suit stops me at every try. The only place I can enter is his lips. I go to kiss them, but he throws me, I've never been thrown so sweetly. I'm flying through the night sky, flying on and on. I keep expecting to hit something but I don't, then I realise something's missing, it's the pain. I say 'What's happening?' Then, from miles away, I hear his voice, so nice to hear again, 'You're dying, you fool, this is how it is.' I say 'Thank you.' He says 'Don't thank me, you little Homo', and then I'm awake and hitting my head off the pillow, and the pain, because it's been gone for a bit, really comes back and has a do . . .

Pause.

. . . and tears me in two.
I must also confesss, Friar Jiggle, that sometimes he's not in

a dream, sometimes he's on the back wall here in the same white gi, sometimes he helps me with the karate machine.

Pause.

What would he say if he saw me now.

He breaks pose.

Oh God.

Friar Jiggle, *who has been engrossed in the work, suddenly looks up to see he's moved off.*

Friar Jiggle   That's okay. Nea' done. Nea' done.

He finishes.

There, all done, you are complete now.

He stands, pleased, holding the pane of glass.

Come. Come. See from here.

Choke *comes round to see it.* **Friar Jiggle** *holds it up in the light beam coming from the headlamp. The light shines through the colours. It looks amazing. The colours come through and on the face of* **Choke** *as he looks.*

Mrs Kooee (*who has popped her head over*)   It's lubly.

Friar Jiggle   It'll take pride o' place in the Gay window and in years to come like the 1066 tapestry men ull say these was Gays.

Choke *suddenly stamps on flag, light goes off, he takes glass.*

Choke   I can't.

He throws it over wall into back street. Hear it smash to pieces.

Mrs Kooee   That's nasty.
(*To* **Friar Jiggle**.) Friar, never mind, love, never mind.

Choke   I can't let go! Not after all these years.
Get out!
Get out!

or I'll be up there
and have your fat neck.

Mrs Kooee   He doesn't mean it.

Choke   Go.

Friar Jiggle *goes.*

Choke   Shut . . .

Mrs Kooee *suddenly notices.*

Mrs Kooee   It's been open all the time and you . . .

Choke *slams it shut.*

Choke   IT'S SHUT NOW!
Piss off.

Mrs Kooee *squeals and pops down.*

Pause.

Mrs Kooee *pops back up.*

Mrs Kooee   It didn't rattle.

Gate suddenly opens. **Sump** *is there standing in gateway.*

Sump   That's 'cause I'm holding it.
What have you done, Friar's crying, running down the
backs.

Choke   Get out!
Get out!
Get out, you queer.

Sump   You're nowt but a little puff.

Choke   I'll kill ya.

Sump   Come and scratch me eyes out, why don't ya.

Choke   Bastard.

Sump   Short arse.

Choke *charges for him with a battle-cry.*

Mrs Kooee *squeals at the sheer force of it and disappears down behind wall.*

Choke *and* **Sump** *go into a real furious fight.*

They fight fast vicious. It's hard to see what's happening.

Choke *gets him in an armlock, forces him down to the paving stones, a single flower is up between the slabs. He pushes* **Sump**'s *nose right into it.*

Choke   Sniff the flower! Sniff it, you bastard!

Sump *gets free, gets him down, sits astride him, elbows him in the face.* **Choke** *looks trapped but he gets him in a choke from this position using his legs.* **Sump** *has to submit.* **Choke** *rolls him over. Stands up, panting, out of breath. Then holds his side and goes over and leans by the rubble heap.*

Sump *still on ground.*

Sump   You always was the choke man. Even from the bottom you was on top.

They are both silent, panting for a while.
Sump *on the floor then sitting up.*
Sump *stands.*

Sump   I'm sorry, Choke, if I upset you. You must do what you want to. I was only thinking of you.

Choke *says nothing. Wobbles a bit.*

Sump   You all right?

Choke   Let's *randori.*

Sump   Speak English. I was never one for all that eastern speak. If you bosh someone it's a bosh. If you chucks 'em over, there they go. If you practise, you practise.

Choke *nods.*

Almost ceremonially takes **Sump**'s *lapels in a judo beginning,*
Sump *goes more into a wrestler's crouch.*
They stand like this breathing for a while. Then begin.

Mrs Kooee *pops up.*

Mrs Kooee   Seconds away, round two.

Pops down fast.

They 'practice fight' slowly. Going into a lock, a throw, a punch combination, a trap, a roll on the ground then up, beautiful to watch, a rhythm to it, between each lock, strangle, etc . . . when the pain comes on they tap loudly with the hand on the floor or their opponent's body, then move on to next move, this adds to the rhythm.

Between sequences, they often pause, in that pause they sometimes speak before the tap, then move on.

Flowing beautiful under the moonlight, the big man and the little man.

Choke   Just thinking there, remember this one.

Does the technique.

That was one of his favourites, wun it?

Sump   Who?

Choke   Slam Dunk, remember him?

Sump   Bloody hell, aye, Slam Dunk and his mate.

Choke   Oriental Joseph.

Sump   That's him.

Choke   He was good, him, Joe. Jui-jitsu man, went to Japan to beat the Japs at their own game.

Sump   Got off with the grand Soke's daughter. She'd have sex wi' him but wouldn't let him finish so to speak. She'd say 'No ejakuwate', 'No ejakuwate'. He swore it helped him win the championship.

Choke   He was a rum un.

Sump   He was when he come back and eventually pulled the plug, his underpants was like the tray of a pigeon cage for two weeks.

They fight on.

Was he one a the physical culturists?

Choke   Slam Dunk was, Joe wasn't. Very few were. Not even a handful. It took a lot to be accepted. Some pushed weights about a bit and tried to join us, some had 'Health and Strength' delivered, but that weren't it.

Sump   I wasn't one.

Choke   You weren't.

Sump   I never had the time.

Choke   Anyway, you was Yorkshire.

Sump   The white rose.

Choke   The red.

They fight on.

Remember Boot.

Sump   The shin man.

Choke   Cave 'em in with his clogs.

Sump   Auld Lancashire fightin'.
Aye, almost gone now.

They stand with straight backs and kick at each other's shins in lightning-fast combinations for a while.

They break, go to the walls panting.

Quiet except for their panting for quite a while.

*Suddenly **Choke** cries out a little bit then muffles it. Turns into wall.*

Choke   Arrgh.

Sump   You all right?

Choke   It's trying to come again, the pain.

Sump   Shall we stop?

Choke   No, it's better when I fight.

Long, long pause.

Choke *facing wall, one hand on stomach side.*

Sump *looking at him from across the yard.*

Choke (*turns round*)   Come on.

They head for centre of yard.

Last round.

They couple-up and start.

Mrss Kooee *pops up.*

Mrs Kooee   Ding ding.

Pops down fast.

They fight on. **Sump** *gets him good, tries to pin him, but* **Choke***'s up and out and found* **Sump***'s neck then releases him and they're into something else.*

Sump   No one can hold you down.

Choke   The ground's always been my place, partly 'cause I'm so close to it already.

They flow on, fighting, tapping, going.

Choke   I remember my first match, tournaments they call 'em now. I like match. You can walk out of a tournament after a shower, with your sports bag and into the leisure-centre bar. You might not have got out of a match alive. One man matched against another. My mam came. She stopped right at the back. I don't think she really wanted to watch in case her baby was hurt. I didn't really know whether she was there, till someone lifted her on a chair and she could see, then I heard her shouting at the other bloke and screaming for me. My dad never came.

They fight on.

Sump   Did you win?

Choke   Yeah, my opponent was about four times my size. My mam said afterwards, 'I knew you'd win once you was on the ground, you're all the same size on the ground.'

They fight on.

There's allsorts coming at me now. Teenage times. None of the fashion would fit, we had no money for made-to-measure, she was always hacking second-hand suits off at the knee and hemming them up for me. I was such a short arse.

Sump   Choke, what you saying!

They fly round.

Choke   Then I'll never forget those times in the gym, all young men, nearly men.

Sump   In more ways than one.

Choke   The rust on the barbells. Cut and ache in your hands. Ache in your heart.

They fight on.

The blisters you went to bed with.

Sump   I never went to bed with no blisters. Just dirty big blokes and nancies.

Choke   They were good times, weren't they, Sump?

Sump   Oh aye.

Choke   There were bad things happening then as ever, but there was a good too. True good, a 1950s good you don't feel now. It was the last age when there was still a bit the feel of good, like the good of the poor in children's books.

Still fighting.

I'm seeing allsorts as we go, Sump. Me outside the dance hall, listening to the music. I wouldn't go in. Not for years. Saturday night all of us suited up, thin black ties, I'd follow

on after everyone from the pub then hang back. I don't
know why. I could dance and everything. I just stood on me
own. Everyone else inside, all the music muffled. Sometimes
it would even rain. I'd start shadow-boxing between the
bins.

Sump   I was on the doors.

Choke   I'd never do that, teacher Walt wouldn't have it.

Sump   Teacher could sod off for five bob a night plus
pints after.

Choke   I didn't . . .

Sump   Drink, I know.
What did you do?

Choke   Train.

Sump   Aye.

Choke   Never switched off. I'm thinkin' of the factory,
between the machines at butty breaks. Empty. Just me
doing breakfalls up and down. Kicking, punching thin air,
shuffling, the only sound was mine.

There's no quiet like the quiet in a mill when the machines
have stopped and the people's gone. Only perhaps the quiet
of the choke-out after the ring in your ears has stopped and
the ink black begins to run.

Choke, *tear in his eye, almost crying.*

They flow on, more beautiful than ever now.

They fight on, silently for a while.

Sump   Was there a karate machine?

Choke *suddenly swiftly throws him over flat on his back. Winds
him.* **Sump** *can't speak. Dazed. Croaking voiceless now. Also limp in*
Choke*'s hands.*

Choke *sits him up. Gets behind him in strangle position.*

Choke   The choke and strangle. The difference is, with a
choke you can put on pain and then release, with a strangle
you're going out. I know every one.

Starts to swiftly but without pressure go through a number of them.

Some I've made up meself. Teacher Walt even showed me
the secret strangle you can do on yourself. The samurai
could use it if they was cornered, no way out. When they
told me he'd choked on his own vomit, I knew what had
really happened.

Carries on swapping chokes.

This one, no this one. I can't choose, Sump, sorry. (*Carries
on.*) This one. (*Carries on.*) My last fight. The last round ever.
(*Suddenly locks into one.*) Aw, this is the one. A deep sleeper.

Sump *coming round more now. Starts shaking his head.* **Choke**
puts the pressure on. **Sump** *begins to go.* **Choke** *suddenly kisses*
Sump *full on the lips just before unconsciousness. Then lets him go to*
sleep.

Choke *lays him gently out on the floor.*

Choke *goes to corner, shadowed, half seen in moonlight. Puts a*
strangle hold on himself, hands round neck, thumbs on points around
throat. Then presses, presses, head falls forward and into wall. He
slides down it.

Blackout.

Lights up. Backyard.

Skip there. Couple of **Men** *in overalls throwing bits of the junk pile in.*

Sump *there in black suit and tie. Watching it go. Picks something up*
looks at it, throws it in skip.

Mrs Kooee*'s head appears over wall. She is also in black.*

Mrs Kooee (*to* **Men**)   There's some tea here if you want it, lads, and bacon.

The two **Men** *stop working and go round.*

It was a nice send-off.

Sump   Only two of us there. I thought some of the others might have turned up, but he'd had no contact with anyone for years. People thought he'd died years ago. I didn't talk about him much to people. He never told you anything so there was nothing much to say really.

Mrs Kooee   I thought I saw Friar Jiggle among the stones.

Sump   You might well have. He watches over his parishioners.

Pause.

Won't be the same now. Think I'll pack it in. I'm getting too old now anyway.

Throws slow punch at last bit of standing apparatus, catches it before it collapses.

Everything was wrong he tried to make. His dad made things, repaired things, I think that's where he got it. But Choke couldn't do it, he just didn't have the knack, but he had these fancies, fancies that led to delusions at the end, poor little sod. Same with the herbs, he didn't really know what he was doing. Probably wrong what he took, probably poison.

Mrs Kooee   But you couldn't tell him.

Sump   The karate machine.

They smile.

He was so on his own. We were both alone, but I never needed a partner, my partner was life, he had no one. All that training, those hours. Where did it go? There's nothing to show.

Mrs Kooee (*holding back tears*)   I'd a had him. He could a snuggled up in my warm sausage house wi' me.

Sump   I keep thinking, he was a child once. How small he must have been.

Mrs Kooee   I'd a had him in my pinny pocket, took him everywhere wi' me.
All that loving lost.

Sump   He was always fighting, fighting his true self, keeping it away with parry and bloke, choking it out if it got too close.

Mrs Kooee (*puts hand on* **Sump***'s shoulder*)   Let me brew some tea up for you.
And there'll be a brondy in it.

She goes.

Sump *alone.*

He walks past skip to record player, puts grand military music on.

Hears something.

Turns it low.

Then hears nothing.

Then hears somebody behind wall whispering.

Sump *stands to one side of gate.*

Waits.

Gate opens.

Somebody steps in.

Sump *pounces, drags them round, gets them in a strangle.*

It's **Yack**.

It's the cat hat **Sump** *has, thinking it's the head of someone.* **Yack** *squealing, struggling, slips out from under it.*

Yack   It's me, Yack!

Sump   What you doing!

Yack *a bit speechless for once.*

Sump   What you doing? Come to pilfer.

Yack   No, the opposite actually.

Takes his hat back.

Oh, the stuffing's squeezed out of her now.

Sump   Come on, Yack, what you after?

Yack   I've come, come to pay my respects of course and say chow to poor little Chokey and that, and come to beg, beg like anything, I'm begging you, please don't go to the rozzers, Sump. Hear my plea.

Sump   What?

Yack   It was Silver. He didn't know what he was taking, he just took, which is Silver's way, if you know him.

Sump   Eh?

Yack *(calls out)*   Silver.

Yack *pulls gate wider open,* **Silver** *comes in pushing something with a cover over it.* **Silver** *looking shamefaced.*

Yack   What a palaver getting it here. He push, I push, he push, I push.

Mrs Kooee *comes in with tea.*

Yack *(taking it)*   Ooo ta, love.

Mrs Kooee *looks at* **Sump**, **Sump** *shakes his head like it doesn't matter, his attention fixed on the covered thing.*

Sump *looks at* **Mrs Kooee** *she at him.*

Sump *starts to go towards it.*

Yack   Say sorry, Silver.

Silver *just stands there.*

Yack   Go on, say it.

Yack *slaps his arm.*

Sump *pulls cover up a little and peeps.*

Sump   It's okay, go on.

Yack   What? Oh. Did you say go?

Sump   Yes.

Yack   Oh God thank.

Goes up close to **Sump.**

Listen, it wasn't for medical purposes, was it? I was fearful we'd contributed to poor little Chokey Choke's demise, so to speak, and such like, in some way. It don't bear thinking about.

Sump   No. No, it wasn't.

Yack   Oh, what a reliefer.

Sump   Go on now, go.

Yack (*happy now*)   Want a tea cosy, Missus?

Holding out cat hat.

Mrs Kooee   No ta.

Yack (*tosses it in skip. To cat hat*)   That's definitely your last life gone.

Yack *and* **Silver** *go. Hear* **Yack** *jabbering as they go.*

Sump *and* **Mrs Kooee** *look at it.*

Sump *and* **Mrs Kooee** *alone.*

Mrs Kooee   Is it?

Sump   I think it is.

They look at it in silence. Music still playing, can be heard.

Sump *goes to it. Whips the sheet off in one. It is a magnificent-looking machine. Shining, beautiful. Pistons and grips sticking out at different angles, chains, parts, cogs gleaming. The Karate Machine.*

They look at it.

Sump *walks round it.*

Sump   Shall I turn it on?

Mrs Koee   Turn it on, Sump.

Sump *goes for starter pull.*

Pulls it.

Nothing.

Pulls it.

Nothing.

Pulls it.

Nothing.

Desperate, tries again, pulls it as hard as he can.

Nothing.

Long, long pause.

Mrs Koee   It don't work.

Sump   No.

Mrs Koee   Oh Chokey, Chokey, Chokey.

Sump *goes and stands with her. They look at machine, put arms round each other and walk to back gate.*

Mrs Kooee *looks back.*

Mrs Koee   What shall we do with it?

Sump *doesn't look back, lets his head fall forward.*

Sump   Tell the men to dump it.

They are gone.

Stage empty.

Machine on its own.

Suddenly machine starts up.

We watch it, it's beautiful, precision engineering in motion. Smooth. Makes a good sound. Pistons to hold. Rods coming in and out in rhythm. Amazing.

The lights dim around it, to a spotlight on it. The music still playing. We watch it in its fascinating operation.

Suddenly, the men come in, in the dark we can hardly see them. They pick up record player and a couple more things and throw them in skip, music screeches and stops.

Pick machine up between them and throw it in skip. Lights down on them.

Only skip, sound of machine in skip. Horrible sound. Knocking off the iron. Whirring, battering.

Blackout.

Nothing in the darkness but this sound.

Whirrs down, then gone.

Silence.

Methuen Modern Plays

include work by

Jean Anouilh
John Arden
Margaretta D'Arcy
Peter Barnes
Sebastian Barry
Brendan Behan
Dermot Bolger
Edward Bond
Bertolt Brecht
Howard Brenton
Anthony Burgess
Simon Burke
Jim Cartwright
Caryl Churchill
Noël Coward
Lucinda Coxon
Sarah Daniels
Nick Darke
Nick Dear
Shelagh Delaney
David Edgar
David Eldridge
Dario Fo
Michael Frayn
John Godber
Paul Godfrey
David Greig
John Guare
Peter Handke
David Harrower
Jonathan Harvey
Iain Heggie
Declan Hughes
Terry Johnson
Sarah Kane
Charlotte Keatley
Barrie Keeffe
Howard Korder

Robert Lepage
Stephen Lowe
Doug Lucie
Martin McDonagh
John McGrath
Terrence McNally
David Mamet
Patrick Marber
Arthur Miller
Mtwa, Ngema & Simon
Tom Murphy
Phyllis Nagy
Peter Nichols
Joseph O'Connor
Joe Orton
Louise Page
Joe Penhall
Luigi Pirandello
Stephen Poliakoff
Franca Rame
Mark Ravenhill
Philip Ridley
Reginald Rose
David Rudkin
Willy Russell
Jean-Paul Sartre
Sam Shepard
Wole Soyinka
Shelagh Stephenson
C. P. Taylor
Theatre de Complicite
Theatre Workshop
Sue Townsend
Judy Upton
Timberlake Wertenbaker
Roy Williams
Victoria Wood

Methuen Contemporary Dramatists
include

Peter Barnes (three volumes)
Sebastian Barry
Edward Bond (six volumes)
Howard Brenton
  (two volumes)
Richard Cameron
Jim Cartwright
Caryl Churchill (two volumes)
Sarah Daniels (two volumes)
Nick Darke
David Edgar (three volumes)
Ben Elton
Dario Fo (two volumes)
Michael Frayn (two volumes)
Paul Godfrey
John Guare
Peter Handke
Jonathan Harvey
Declan Hughes
Terry Johnson (two volumes)
Bernard-Marie Koltès
David Lan
Bryony Lavery
Doug Lucie
David Mamet (three volumes)

Martin McDonagh
Duncan McLean
Anthony Minghella
  (two volumes)
Tom Murphy (four volumes)
Phyllis Nagy
Anthony Nielsen
Philip Osment
Louise Page
Joe Penhall
Stephen Poliakoff
  (three volumes)
Christina Reid
Philip Ridley
Willy Russell
Ntozake Shange
Sam Shepard (two volumes)
Wole Soyinka (two volumes)
David Storey (three volumes)
Sue Townsend
Michel Vinaver (two volumes)
Michael Wilcox
David Wood (two volumes)
Victoria Wood

Methuen World Classics
include

Jean Anouilh (two volumes)
John Arden (two volumes)
Arden & D'Arcy
Brendan Behan
Aphra Behn
Bertolt Brecht (six volumes)
Büchner
Bulgakov
Calderón
Čapek
Anton Chekhov
Noël Coward (seven volumes)
Eduardo De Filippo
Max Frisch
John Galsworthy
Gogol
Gorky
Harley Granville Barker
  (two volumes)
Henrik Ibsen (six volumes)
Lorca (three volumes)

Marivaux
Mustapha Matura
David Mercer (two volumes)
Arthur Miller (five volumes)
Molière
Musset
Peter Nichols (two volumes)
Clifford Odets
Joe Orton
A. W. Pinero
Luigi Pirandello
Terence Rattigan
  (two volumes)
W. Somerset Maugham
  (two volumes)
August Strindberg
  (three volumes)
J. M. Synge
Ramón del Valle-Inclán
Frank Wedekind
Oscar Wilde